FESTIVE TARTS

FESTIVE TARTS

Splendid Fare for Fun and Fanciful Occasions

BY *Sylvia Thompson*

ILLUSTRATED BY *Brooke Scudder*

CHRONICLE BOOKS
SAN FRANCISCO

For Alice Vinegar,
my grandmother, in whose kitchen I discovered
the pleasures of baking.

Library of Congress Cataloging-in-Publication Data available.

✳

Designed by Aufuldish & Warinner
Printed in Hong Kong

✳

ISBN 0-8118-0720-7

✳

Distributed in Canada by
Raincoast Books
8680 Cambie St., Vancouver, B.C. V6P 6M9

✳

10 9 8 7 6 5 4 3 2 1

✳

Chronicle Books
275 Fifth Street, San Francisco, CA 94103

✳

Contents

Acknowledgments

Tarts are fun-and-a-half to make. They're especially fun when you're creating them, trying now this combination of flavors and textures, now that composition of colors and shapes. But no one creates in a vacuum.

✳

My mother—Alice Vinegar's daughter—and friends Lynnda Hart, Hildegard Manley, Jane Levy, and Norah Barr have been wonderfully generous with their time and gifts. I've also been inspired by Myrtle Allen, Phineas Beck, Marcel Boulestin, Bernard Clayton, Jr., Jim Dodge, Elizabeth David, the *Farm Journal's Pie Cookbook,* Bo Friberg, Deborah Madison, Richard Olney, Elisabeth Orsini, Russ Parsons, Helen Perrin, Lulu Peyraud, Susan Purdy, Nancy Silverton, Catherine Turney, Alice Waters, Andrew and Susie Schwartz, and Paula Wolfert.

✳

Mary Ann Gilderbloom, Marie Hall, Cindy Pukatch, Dolores Sizer, Marion Siwek, Caitlin Szieff, and Nan Wollman have baked tarts for me, and every recipe has come back brighter.

✳

"So what are you making for supper?" "A tart of our Northstar cherries with chocolate crumbles." "Sounds like a book to me!" Susan Lescher continues to nurture me in the world of books and out.

✳

Bill LeBlond and Leslie Jonath make writing a Chronicle Book even more fun than making tarts. Sharon Silva deserves a medal for valor in copy editing. Brooke Scudder! Once again her brilliance illumines my words to a fare-thee-well.

✳

Finally, were it not for my incomparable husband, you would not hold this book in your hands.
I am profoundly grateful.

✳

The Edible Plate

In their earliest appearances—around the eleventh century—tarts were dinner plates. Knights of the Middle Ages plucked their morsels of "tendre gees" or bit of "deynte fyssche" from a trencher. To the Norman knights, a trencher was usually a hollowed-out loaf or a flat disk-shaped piece of bread. When the meal was over, they nibbled at the crusty plate, enjoying all that sauce-sopped bread. By the thirteenth century, somebody had the bright idea of eating the dinner plate and its contents at the same time. The tart was born. During the Renaissance, banqueting in Italy flowered on the tables of the Medicis of Florence. In the sixteenth century, young Caterina de' Medici married into the French royal family and part of her dowry were the chefs she brought along. It was Caterina's cooks who served a sweet dish at the end of a meal for the first time in Paris. A century before, for example, a favorite French tart—served with the meat course—was a crustade ryal (royal custard), made of beef marrow mixed with sugar, almonds, spices, currants, and dates. Now the idea of having a sweet final touch to dining caught the

French imagination, and the great line of French tarts began.

Soon, across the Channel, the English were satisfying the national sweet tooth with "strobarye tairtes" and Good Queen Bess's favorite, "march pane," tarts of marzipan.

Back in American colonial days, we had no time for tarts. Life was hard in the new country. Colonial children were expected to eat their supper standing up and in silence. Dinner was served on wooden trenchers, and after meat and vegetables from "the dinner side," a Puritan turned his trencher over to "the pie side."

Came the Revolution. When France joined the colonists' side, an enthusiastic burst of Francophilia swept through the kitchens of young America. President Thomas Jefferson sent to Paris for his chef. All sorts of French dishes turned up on colonial tables. A shell of French puff paste might, for a Virginia dessert, enclose not a filling of *fraises des bois chantilly*, but whole native Virginia pecans in home-refined cane syrup gilded with rum.

There were tarts in the new West, too. In her diary in 1841, Mrs. Mary Walker, whose missionary husband was out in the wilds of the Oregon Territory, wrote: "Thurs. 11 Fried two big pans of cakes. Baked two ovens full of bread and plenty of tarts. Hope husband will smell them and come where they are."

As the country was being enriched by immigrants, so was American cuisine. Germans brought their delicious baking with them, and a turn-of-the-century Maifest was celebrated with tarts of sour cream and raisins, lemon cream, peaches and nuts, and anything else they could lay their light-hands-with-pastry upon.

So, what began as a trencher had evolved into a round flat pastry that held a filling—a tart was a shell with a dinner-plate air about it. A pie? A pie is nothing but a tart with a hat on. Tarts can wear hats as well, though few do.

A big difference between a pie and a tart is that a tart is presented on its own—no pan. Because a tart shell is an independent matter, bakers give it due consideration. Often the pastry is first baked separately, then the filling is added. This ensures that both pastry and filling are cooked perfectly.

Form follows function, and since the pastry must stand on its own, a tart's sides are shorter than a pie's—a mere inch. Therefore, the main distinction between a pie and a tart is its depth. Somehow on the whole, tarts seem richer, more interesting than pies. I think that's because we're tempted to compress as much flavor and enjoyment into that inch as we can. Savory ingredients are particularly good in a tart shell—as they were in the beginning.

So consider tarts as festive edible plates filled with imagination. And if you don't have a festive occasion to hand, invent one to match your tart!

How to Make a perfect tart

A Few Terms in This Book

BITTERSWEET CHOCOLATE. Not altogether sweet, not altogether bitter, bittersweet chocolate has considerably more character than semisweet chocolate (it contains more chocolate essence). If domestic bittersweet chocolate isn't at your supermarket, you'll find it, European made, at fancy groceries or confectioneries.

BLIND. Baking a tart shell blind means baking it without filling.

CRISP. Crisp pastry has the texture of a sugar cookie; generally it is used with fillings that would make more delicate pastries soggy.

EGG WASH. Beaten whole egg or egg yolk with a pinch of salt. It is used as a moisture barrier on the bottom of a tart shell, or brushed on dough so it will burnish in baking.

FLAKY. A flaky pastry feels in the mouth as though it is composed of countless flaky layers—and it may be!

FLAN. In France, the word is, to all intents and purposes, interchangeable with *tarte;* in Spain, a *flan* is a custard.

FLUTE. To finish the border of a tart or pie with ruffles or pinches.

FRAISAGE. This technique, which is used in preparing crisp pastry dough, forces all ingredients, especially fat and flour, to blend intimately.

Use the heel of your hand to smear walnut-sized pieces of dough across about 6 inches of the counter, as you straighten your arm. When you're finished, scrape the dough together and pat and press it until it holds together.

PULSE. A term for the food processor that means to flick the machine on/off, on/off so it runs a fraction of a second at each flick. You have control this way and there is less danger of over-processing; you can do the same with a blender.

SHELL. The pastry case of a tart.

SHORT. In the mouth, short pastry dissolves into a sweet, melting almost-crunch.

SOFTENED VERSUS ROOM-TEMPERATURE BUTTER. Room temperature butter is at 70°F—malleable but on the firm side. Softened butter is almost the consistency of mayonnaise. Fine points, but fine points make fine baking.

SUGAR SYRUP. A light syrup for general use is 1 cup sugar dissolved in 1 cup water and brought to a simmer. You can poach fruit in it at once, or simmer it 5 to 10 minutes for a thicker consistency. It will keep indefinitely in the refrigerator.

The Tart Baker's Makes-It-Easy Equipment List

A BIG—BIG!—AND PLEASING BOWL. By hand is the most sensuous way to make pastry.

And it's fun! It's not fun if your hands are cramped in a small bowl and the flour's flying all over the place. Tarts are luxurious matters, and you want a feeling of opulence. So even though you're working with ingredients for just one tart, use a great big bowl.

WEIGHTS AND MEASURES. Use a clear pitcher for liquids and nested cups for dry ingredients, and look for the sliding teaspoon and tablespoon measures.

A CHOPSTICK. For smoothing off dry ingredients lightly spooned into a measuring cup.

A SMOOTH AND AMPLE WORK SURFACE. It should be lower than your waist (so you won't strain your shoulders and back) as you mix and knead. Marble is ideal because it helps keep dough cool, but a wooden tabletop is excellent.

A ROLLING PIN. You need one that fits you like a glove. Early Americans used (and many Europeans still use) a piece of wooden broom handle.

I'm lucky to have my husband's grandmother's, and I'm constantly surprised at how much control I have with such a simple tool. A rolling pin whose barrel turns effortlessly around the handles, such as those that contain ball bearings, also have its place.

A SMOOTH DISH TOWEL OR LARGE PIECE OF CANVAS. Sprinkle it with flour, rub the flour in, and roll out your pastry. Dough will never stick.

A STOCKINETTE SLEEVE. This slips onto your rolling pin and cuts down on the flour you'll need for rolling; the more flour, the tougher the pastry. Look for one in a kitchen supply store.

A RULER. You'll need one.

A MARKED TOOTHPICK. For a quick gauge, mark off ⅛, ³⁄₁₆, and ¼ inch with indelible ink on a toothpick. As you roll, stand the toothpick

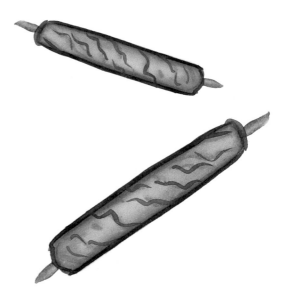

in the dough here and there to instantly check the thickness.

A TART PAN. It has two parts: a straight-sided fluted ring with a bottom lip that supports a round base that lifts out. Straight sides give the tart not only nobility but strength. The rounded fluting isn't just decorative, it increases the strength. The moment the tart is baked, you remove the base from the ring. Unless the pastry or filling is too fragile, the tart is then slid off the base onto a rack to cool or a platter to serve. A tart standing on its own is not only aesthetic, but no metal holds steam against the crust, inviting sog. Yet when you do need a base to support the tart, it can be there. It's invisible until you serve the tart, then, who cares?

A TART (OR FLAN) RING. This inch-high metal hoop, plain or fluted, is placed on a baking sheet with one rimless side or on an upside-down rimmed baking sheet. You use the pair as a tart pan, the difference being there's no base to support a fragile tart. You slide the ring off the sheet rather than lift it.

A STURDY ROUND, SQUARE, OR RECTANGULAR MOLD OF FOIL. To fashion a mold, fold two sheets of heavy 18-inch aluminum foil into a strip 1 inch wide (it will be a scant ⅛ inch thick). To determine the length you need for a round tart, multiply the diameter by 3.1416 (pi). For a strip to mold a square or rectangular tart, measure the length of the four sides, add them together, and then add 1 inch in length to any strip you cut. Mold the strip around something the size and shape you want, slip one end into the inch-long cuff of the other end, and staple or pin securely. Carefully handled, foil molds can be used again and again.

TARTLET PANS. These come in a mishmosh of sizes and shapes, none of them standard. If you don't have any and don't expect to make tartlets often, form shells by molding your dough over the back of the cups of a muffin pan. Remember that tartlets are as shallow as tarts—if not shallower—so mold the pastry to make it an inch deep. I happen to own pans that are 4 inches in diameter and 1 inch deep, and some that are 20 inches in diameter. They're what I call for in my recipes. Both sizes are available from well-stocked cookware shops.

SHARP SCISSORS. For trimming the edge of dough. A knife can pull it, and stretching dough is a no-no.

A PASTRY BRUSH. For spreading butter, mustard, or egg yolk on the pastry. From a hardware store's paint section, choose the cheapest brush that's flat, supple, and an inch or so wide. A sturdy feather also makes a good brush.

PIE WEIGHTS. These are what hold the dough down while it's baking blind. You can invest in aluminum or china weights that will last a lifetime, or you can simply use dried beans and keep them with your baking things. Be sure you lay a sheet of waxed paper in the shell before adding the weights, or you'll be picking them out of the pastry.

A BIG PIZZA PAN OR BAKING SHEET. One of these is needed for the tart pan or mold to bake on. This provides even distribution of heat for the tart, and keeps any spills from the oven floor.

A BAKING STONE. Heated hot, a stone makes flaky pastry flakier because the faster pastry bakes, the higher it rises.

A COOLING RACK. A metal grid on feet that permits air to circulate under the pastry, allowing it to crispen. A rack from a restaurant supply won't be too big: when you give the tart a push, it won't slide onto the rack—and then off!

A LONG, STURDY METAL SPATULA. This separates the tart from its base and helps scoot the tart onto the cooling rack. One from a restaurant supply is recommended.

A BIG, BROAD PANCAKE TURNER. This helps slide the tart smoothly from cooling rack to platter.

A LARGE, FLAT SERVING PLATTER OR TRAY. Essential for presenting these beauties, the dish or tray should be at least 2 inches wider than the tart—4 to 6 inches is better. (Until you find the perfect service, you can set the tart on pretty cloth napkins on the pizza pan or baking sheet.)

SERVING UTENSILS. You'll need two implements, something to cut the slice and something broad and wedge-shaped to slide under the slice, free it, and lift it intact. Give priority to tools that work rather than to their decorative value.

Ingredients: What Does What in Pastry

FAT, I'm afraid, is what makes pastry so appealing. It gives the silkiness, the sweetness, the crunch. How much fat is contained in each serving of these tarts? On average, about the same as in a serving of real ice cream.

BUTTER is numero uno for flavor. A friend asked, Why use unsalted butter and then add salt to the dough? *Unsalted butter* is invariably fresh. Salt preserves butter, permitting it to be stored. You might not perceive stored butter until it was baked into your pastry—heat brings out flavor molecules—and then you'd go gaaah! All-butter pastry is crispier and firmer than pastry made with lard and shortening.

LARD makes the sweetest, shortest pastry of all. Packaged lard is better than none, but when you can, buy a pound or two of leaf lard, cut it into small pieces, and effortlessly melt it in a pan in a 300°F oven. It keeps in the refrigerator for months.

PURE VEGETABLE SHORTENING, to my mind, is preferable to margarine as a substitute for animal fats in pastry. Even quality stick margarines—which you can use—contain a bunch of preserving thises and thats. Shortening is second to lard in giving delectably textured pastry.

WHICH FLOUR TO USE? Read five baking books and you'll read five opinions as to which flour makes the best pastry (and you'll get opinions that differ from mine on all sorts of aspects of baking). After trying them all in every combination, I

find high-gluten *unadulterated bread flour* (the choice of most baking professionals) makes sublime pastries. All-purpose flour can be substituted.

CORNMEAL For a crunchy contrast in your tart shell, make it with *cornmeal*. Blue cornmeal gives maximum flavor. Dried blue corn kernels are available at many health-food stores and they'll grind them for you. Ask for *flour*—not meal—fineness. If blue corn or even dried yellow corn isn't close by, use packaged cornmeal, either yellow or white, and grind it to flour in a blender.

SEMOLINA is hard wheat, the grits left in the machine after the fine flour has been removed. It makes a delicious crunchy crust.

SEA SALT is more deeply flavored than earth salt, and you can buy it without preservatives. To substitute earth salt, use a little more.

A LITTLE BAKING POWDER, of course, adds lift—just enough to let air flow through the pastry in baking, which causes it to bake evenly and thoroughly, and thus prevent soggy pockets.

ICE WATER makes pastry light.

HEAVY CREAM makes pastry richer, darker, and even lighter than water.

MILK can be used instead of cream for a less dramatic effect.

EGG YOLK adds richness and flavor.

A LITTLE ACID such as cider vinegar (distilled white vinegar is too harsh), fresh lemon juice, orange juice, or white wine is a trick our grandmothers used to relax the dough quickly and help make the pastry tender.

STORE-BOUGHT PASTRY? It will serve if it must and you use prime-quality *refrigerated dough*. Do not use frozen dough, as it can shatter.

Amounts

WHAT'S THE BEST SIZE FOR A TART? Eleven inches is standard with most chefs. It gives 8 servings unless the filling is ultrarich, and then it could serve as many as 12.

However, I bake all my tarts in an 11½ incher. The extra ½ inch gives the same number of servings, but they seem more generous than by rights a ½ inch would provide. Remember: you must give seconds. Eight servings of a superb savory tart is safest for 4 people, and of a sweet tart, 6 people at most.

ADAPTING AMOUNTS OF FILLING TO OTHER TART-PAN SIZES. Fillings in these recipes are designed for an 11½-inch-round, 1-inch-deep, straight-sided tart pan. To fit in an 11-inch pan, make a border that raises the sides ⅛ inch.

By the same token, an 8-by-1-inch tart pan accommodates a half recipe of both dough and filling.

If your straight-sided round pan is considerably bigger or smaller, pull out your calculator. Multiply 3.1416 (pi) times half your pan's diameter times half your pan's diameter (the latter is not a misprint) times its depth. The number for my 11½-inch pan is 103.87. *To increase an ingredient*, divide the larger pan's number by the smaller to get the percentage of difference, then multiply

the ingredient by that much for the amount to use. *To decrease an ingredient,* divide the smaller pan's number by the larger to get the percent of difference, then multiply the ingredient by that number for the amount. Regarding the pan sizes, we're talking about cylinders. The formula won't be accurate with slope-sided pie pans, but often the relative percentages will work. Kitchen math is the only math that's fun.

CONVERTING A PIE RECIPE INTO A TART RECIPE. Most recipes for a 9-by-1½-inch pie dish will fit into an 11- to 11½-inch tart shell.

Tricks of the Trade

MAKE EVERY STEP BRIEF. Whether you're working by hand or machine, the less any dough is handled, the better. If you're new to making pastry, get the feel of it by using a machine. The process will go more quickly.

KEEP COOL. If the weather is hot, make pastry in the coolest spot you can find. Warmth tends to make things gluey.

MEASURE THE FLOUR AND OTHER DRY INGREDIENTS ACCURATELY. Spoon it lightly into the measuring cup, then sweep off the excess with a chopstick or pencil.

HAVE THE FAT SUPPLE—NEARLY SOFT. This way, the fat blends with the flour and the dough quickly pulls together. Cold fat stays suspended, and you'll have to add liquid to make a dough. The less liquid, the shorter and lighter the pastry.

FOR SHORT AND FLAKY PASTRY, KEEP FAT PIECES LARGE. As the pieces of fat in the dough melt in baking, the places where they were when solid become pockets of air, creating lightness in the pastry.

TO ROLL OUT THE DOUGH. Sprinkle a smooth dish towel or large piece of canvas with flour and rub it in. If you have one, slip a stockinette sleeve onto your rolling pin—or lay waxed paper on top of the dough—and roll out (lift the paper off from time to time to uncrinkle it). Rotate the dough occasionally so it will be even, and add as little flour as you can to the cloth, always brushing off the excess. Measure the thickness from time to time with a marked toothpick (page 10). Make the round, square, or rectangle as even as you can, patching as needed.

TO PATCH THE DOUGH. Fit pieces together and gently roll, press, or pinch to seal the seam. Do not use water for glue. Keep the trimmings handy in case you need to patch the dough when baking. When you're baking a shell blind—either partially or fully—check before it's supposed to be finished for cracks and holes. If you find any, smooth just a veil of dough over the gap and bake until it cooks.

TO FIT THE DOUGH INTO THE MOLD. Set the unbuttered pan or baking sheet with its ring at the edge of the towel, close to you. Hold your rolling pin over the center of the rolled-out dough. Lift the corner of the towel closest to you and the mold until half the dough falls over the

pin. Drop the towel, lift the dough, and quickly slide the mold under the dough, centering it. Holding it over the pan, let the dough fall and settle of its own weight into the bottom. You may have to wiggle the mold a little, or gently lift the dough here and there, but be careful not to stretch the dough. Stretching dough makes it shrink more than it needs to in baking, so ease the dough into the mold's nooks and crannies. *Big* sigh of relief! Now use your fingers to press the dough in place. Take care to press it firmly into the angle where the sides and bottom meet. Smooth out any bubbles. Press the dough into the sides.

TO TRIM THE DOUGH. When the dough is snug in the mold, arrange the excess so it falls evenly over the top of the ring. Using sharp scissors, snip along the *outside* even with the rim, unless otherwise directed. If you're in a hurry and this is a casual tart, you can simply roll your pin over the top of the mold and, in one sweep, all excess will be cut off. But the first way gives you a tad more pastry, so when it shrinks in baking, the sides aren't skimpy.

A DECORATIVE BORDER? Unless I need to make the sides taller, or the sides of the mold aren't fluted, I skip this step. With its splendid filling, the tart's gorgeous aplenty. If you want to add a decorative border, allow for a 1½-inch margin on all sides. Trim, leaving a ½-inch overhang around the outside of the rim. Fold the dough down onto itself inside the shell, either flush with the top of the rim or rising a little above it. Flute,

pinch, or press around the rim as you like.

TO MAKE FREEFORM SHELLS. Most of the recipes in this book call for using a tart mold or ring simply because it's easiest. If you're a free spirit, you'll want to make tart shells of your own design—rectangular, square, teardrop, star, figure-8, whatever moves you. Nowhere is it written a tart must conform, and freeform shapes are enormously festive. Your only concern will be getting the sides to stay up. The secret lies in double or triple walls. Using the appropriate margin, fold the dough over one or two times—once for Crisp Sweet Pastry (page 24), twice for Short Crust Pastry (page 22)—to make inch-high walls of several thicknesses.

For a rectangle to stand, firmly pinch the corners. For a rounded form, pleat and pinch the sides. Press gently all around to amalgamate the layers. Until you know how your dough will behave, it's wise to use a broad band of aluminum foil (page 11) on the outside for support. Make a foil tent of several thicknesses, set it over the sides, and pleat and pinch as you did the dough to give it a second skin. Chill well and partially or fully bake as usual. I don't recommend using Flaky Pastry (page 23) for a freeform because it has a flyaway mind of its own.

TO DETERMINE HOW MUCH FILLING YOUR UNBAKED FREEFORM SHELL WILL NEED, fit doubled food-storage bags inside the shell. Fill with water to the top of the shell, then lift out the bags and measure the water. You may need more than one double bag.

MOISTUREPROOFING THE BOTTOM OF THE TART SHELL. You can keep the bottom crust from getting soggy by brushing it with a light impenetrable coating of Dijon mustard, egg wash, or melted unsalted butter, jam, jelly, or chocolate—whatever is most appropriate to the filling. If there's to be a really juicy fruit filling, cover the bottom with a thin layer of sponge cake before adding the fruit.

REHEATING A PREBAKED SHELL. You can warm the pastry slowly and gently in a barely warm oven (250°F), or heat it fast when the oven's hot (375°F). Just keep an eye on it and set the shell on a pizza pan or baking sheet.

TO BAKE A FILLED TART—WHETHER WITH RAW DOUGH OR BAKED PASTRY. Heat the oven, moistureproof the shell, arrange the filling, and bake as directed in the recipe. Remove the rim (unless instructed otherwise). If the tart is to be served cold, leave it on the rack. If it is to be served hot, center it on the platter, set it down, then quickly pull away the base or leave it there.

TO UNMOLD A TART. See steps 17 through 19 on page 18.

TO MOVE A TART FROM THE COOLING RACK TO ITS SERVING PLATTER. Center the tart over the platter. If the tart is firm enough, just tip the rack and let the tart slide onto the plate. If the tart is fragile, use a broad pancake turner to support the tart on one side as you tip the rack and slide the tart onto the plate, then gently pull away the pancake turner.

BAKING AT HIGH ALTITUDE (AROUND 5,000 FEET). Bake at about 15 degrees higher than directed in the recipe.

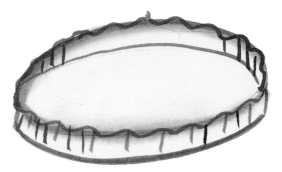

10 Easy Steps to Preparing Perfect Short and Crisp Pastries

MIXING IN A FOOD PROCESSOR:

1. In the bowl, combine the dry ingredients (if used, fruit zest is included) and pulse a few times to blend.

2. Cut the fat into the bowl in thin ½-inch chips or small blobs.

3. Pulse until most fat pieces are the size of large peas, about 10 times.

4. Turn the liquid ingredient(s) into a measuring pitcher—if there is more than one liquid, blend them together with a fork.

5. Sprinkle the liquid over the bowl. Pulse just until the mixture becomes a mass of crumbles, about 6 times. Turn onto your work surface.

MIXING BY HAND:

1. In a big mixing bowl, blend the dry ingredients

(if used, fruit zest is included) with your hands.

2. Cut the fat into the bowl in thin ½-inch chips or small blobs.

3. Moving briskly around the bowl, rub the fat and flour together with your fingertips until most of the fat pieces are the size of large peas, about 3 minutes.

4. Turn the liquid ingredient(s) into a salt shaker. If there is more than one liquid, shake it to blend. If egg is involved, use a measuring pitcher and blend with a fork.

5. As you sprinkle the liquid over the bowl, use a fork to press moistened crumbles together, then drop as much as sticks to the fork onto your work surface. Continue until all the liquid is blended into all the flour.

TO CONTINUE, FOR EITHER METHOD:

6. Pat the crumbles as best you can into a ½-inch-thick round. Don't knead them together and don't worry. If you are making crisp pastry, now do the *fraisage* (page 9).

7. If there's time, wrap the round in aluminum foil and let the dough relax in the refrigerator's crisper 15 to 30 minutes. It can rest for up to 24 hours like this, if convenient. If cold, bring to cool room temperature before rolling it out.

8. Roll out the dough ⅛ inch thick in the shape of the mold, making sure it extends at least 2 inches wider than the mold's diameter.

9. Fit the dough into the mold, then trim the edges around the outside of the mold. Set a tart pan on a pizza pan or baking sheet.

10. Set in the freezer for 15 minutes or the refrigerator for 30 minutes before baking according to the recipe.

10 More Easy Steps: Prebaking Blind Tart Shells of Short, Flaky, Crisp, and Hazelnut Pastries

11. Moistureproof the bottom of the unbaked shell with something appropriate to the filling (page 16).

12. Line the bottom with a square or two of waxed paper. Fill with pie weights ½ inch deep.

13. Position a rack in the middle of the oven (unless otherwise directed); if you have a baking stone, put it on the rack. Heat the oven to 400°F.

14. Set the pizza pan or baking sheet holding the mold on the baking stone or directly on the oven rack.

15. Bake 15 minutes without opening the oven door, then remove from the oven. Using hot pads, lift out the weights; if the dough has ballooned up, prick it with a table fork in a dozen places. If patching is needed, do it now (page 14). Return the mold on its baking sheet to the oven.

16. *For a partially baked shell,* bake until the dough looks firm and no longer raw, about 5 more minutes. (Tart shells for custards and other wet fillings should be fully baked.) Remove from the oven and skip steps 17 through 19. Cool a partially baked shell in the mold. *For a fully baked shell,* once the weights are removed, bake

until golden, 12 to 15 more minutes. Check every 3 to 4 minutes in the beginning to see whether you need to prick the dough again. Remove from the oven and unmold.

17. Center a two-part tart pan on top of a broad, sturdy can. Pull back your hands and the ring will fall to the counter. Holding the tart from underneath, carefully slide it onto the cooling rack.

18. Unless the pastry or filling is fragile and needs the support of the mold's base, run a spatula between the tart and the base, nudging it off the base onto the cooling rack. If the tart is between firm and fragile, take hold of as much of the tart pan's base as you can with both hands, and pull it out fast. If it's very fragile, leave it on the base.

19. For the ring on a baking sheet, use a long metal spatula to free the pastry from the pan, then tip and slide the tart off onto the rack. Leave the ring in place.

20. If the filling will be cold, let the pastry cool thoroughly before filling.

How to Make Tartlet Shells

Cut the dough 1 inch wider than the mold on all sides. You can line and bake the molds just as you do a large tart, but it's considerably easier—if cruder—to fit the dough over the back of a mold. Pinch the edges evenly as needed to make the dough snug. Moistureproof before filling.

Tartlet shells are almost always fully baked blind. If you have lined the back of the molds, set them upside down on a baking sheet and chill while you heat the oven to 400°F. Bake in the middle of the oven until lightly browned, 10 to 13 minutes. Remove from the oven and lift off the shells—if not too fragile—and cool upside down on a rack. If fragile, cool right side up.

TO MAKE JAM TURNOVERS FROM DOUGH TRIMMINGS. Once the tart has baked enough and you know you'll have no need of dough for patching, press trimmings together and roll into one or more thin rounds or squares of any size you please. Drop a little jam, jelly, or preserves to one side of the center, moisten the rim with a fingertip dipped in water, fold over, and use a fork to press the edges together to seal. Set on a small baking sheet or a cake pan turned upside down and bake on the bottom rack along with the tart until nicely browned, 15 to 20 minutes. Serve warm dusted with confectioners' sugar.

Make-Ahead Notes for Pastries

IN THE REFRIGERATOR (wrapped airtight): All the unshaped raw doughs in this book except flaky pastry keep fresh at least 5 days; rolled out, they keep fresh at least 3 days. Unshaped raw flaky dough keeps fresh 2 to 3 days but only 1 to 2 days after rolling out.

Most unfilled baked pastry shells keep fresh 4 to 5 days.

While a few filled baked tarts are even better the day after baking, most will never have the quality they have fresh from the oven. It's also true that if you don't have a spanking fresh tart to taste it against, some next-day's tarts are wonderful. Refrigerate a baked tart only if there's danger of spoilage. It will keep at least 1 day. Otherwise, it's kinder to all elements if you keep it in one of the following ways:

IN A COOL PLACE: All the unfilled baked pastry shells in this book will keep at least 3 days; baked meringue shells will keep *loosely wrapped* if the air is dry for 1 to 2 weeks.

Baked tarts filled with nonperishable ingredients will keep 1 day, at least.

IN THE FREEZER: All the raw doughs in this book, whether unshaped or rolled out, will keep 2 to 3 months. All unfilled baked pastry shells, except flaky pastry, will keep 4 to 6 weeks.

Some filled baked pastries can be frozen for 2 to 3 weeks, but it's chancy and quality usually suffers.

Tart Shells by Mail Order

For a party, should you wish to fill dozens of tiny tartlet shells but don't have the time or the molds, you can buy rounds and even fish-shaped shells of puff paste and short pastry of excellent quality from Pidy-Belgium. They also offer larger shells, even square *vol-au-vents*. Telephone 800-231-7439 to inquire.

Although each pastry has a character and texture that suits it better to some fillings than others, feel free to make any pastry you'd like for any recipe. Actually, you could make the Short Crust Pastry for every tart you ever made forever and you'd shake your head each time at how good it is.

ALL RECIPES MAKE ONE 11- TO 11½-INCH TART SHELL, ABOUT TWELVE 4-BY-1-INCH TARTLET SHELLS, OR ABOUT SIXTEEN 2½-INCH TARTLET SHELLS.

Recipes in this chapter:

Short Crust Pastry

I've been making short pastry for eons, and this is the best I've ever made.

> 1 ⅔ cups bread flour or all-purpose flour
>
> ⅜ teaspoon baking powder
>
> (¼ plus ⅛ or a rounded ¼ teaspoon)
>
> ½ teaspoon sea salt
>
> 6 tablespoons (3 ounces) lard or
>
> vegetable shortening
>
> 5 tablespoons (2½ ounces) unsalted butter,
>
> softened
>
> 2½ tablespoons ice water
>
> ½ tablespoon cider vinegar

Prepare as described in steps 1 through 10 on page 16.

VARIATION: SHORT WHEATEN PASTRY

Wonderfully light and nutty—and nothing "health foody" about it. Use ⅔ cup whole-wheat flour for ⅔ cup of the bread flour or all-purpose flour in Short Crust Pastry.

VARIATION: SHORT HERBAL PASTRY

You can add enormously to the depth of flavor in a tart by blending any herbs or seeds into the dough that you would add to the filling. Actually, the surprise of finding them in the pastry—always a delayed reaction—makes the tart the more interesting.

Add the flavorings to the flour in Short Crust Pastry or Short Wheaten Pastry. The amount you use depends on their strength of flavor, which has to do not only with their genes, but also with their age and quality. Fresh herbs are minced. Some herbs dry satisfactorily. They're marked with an *. Use only about one-third the amount given of dried leaves, crumbling them in. Be adventurous!

Remembering that everyone perceives flavors a bit differently, here are measurements I find harmonious in a tart. Add slowly, tasting the dough to make sure you've got a balance you like.

1 tablespoon: bay, caraway seeds, celery seeds, cilantro, dill,* fennel seeds, mint,* oregano,* rosemary,* sage, summer savory,* tarragon,* Thai basil, thyme (including lemon thyme).*

1½ tablespoons: lemon and sweet basils, chives, crumbled dried hot chilies (without their seeds), fennel leaves, fines herbes (½ teaspoon each parsley, tarragon, chervil, and chives), flat-leaf parsley, marjoram.*

2 tablespoons: chervil.

Don't forget lemon zest. Although not an herb, it is one of the most elegant and appealing touches of all in pastry. Use 2 tablespoons.

VARIATION: SHORT PARMESAN PASTRY

The addition of Parmesan gives a wonderful oomph to savory fillings that are on the bland side. Just be sure you shred it on the fine blade of the grater.

To the flour in the Short Crust Pastry or Short Wheaten Pastry, add ¾ cup (about 1½ ounces) *freshly finely shredded* Parmesan cheese. Omit the salt. Use vegetable shortening in place of lard. You can also use Cheddar or any other grating cheese you like in Parmesan's place.

Cornmeal or Semolina Pastry

This pastry is light and short, with just enough flavor of the grain to be rich without overpowering. Grind dried corn kernels, cornmeal, or semolina to flour consistency in a blender.

1 cup bread flour or all-purpose flour
⅔ cup corn flour (start with 1½ ounces
*   kernels) or semolina flour*
Rounded ¼ teaspoon sea salt
½ cup vegetable shortening, softened
5 tablespoons ice water

Prepare as described in steps 1 through 10 on pages 16 and 17. (This dough can be crumbly, but patch and pat it together as needed when rolling it out and fitting it in the mold, and don't worry.) To bake partially, moistureproof it, then line it with waxed paper and pie weights. Bake in a preheated oven at 425°F for 8 minutes; remove the weights and bake until crisp, about 8 minutes more. To bake completely, continue until nicely browned, about 6 minutes more. Let cool.

Flaky Pastry

Aka quick puff paste or demi-puff paste, this takes more time to make than short crust, but it's worth every minute. This simplified puff pastry has 729 layers when it's baked. It may not rise as high as classic puff pastry, but you'll find nothing *demi* about its lightness. The British call this flaky pastry. It's incredible.

Although you can cheat on the 30 minutes' resting between steps, the resting and chilling make a big difference in the delicacy of the finished pastry, so don't.

1½ cups bread flour
½ teaspoon sea salt
12 tablespoons (6 ounces) unsalted butter, cool
*   but supple, cut into ½-inch squares each ¼*
*   inch thick*
¼ cup cold heavy cream

Although you can make it in a food processor, this dough is best worked by hand, since you don't want the pieces of butter to be blended into the flour. The butter should be colder than for short dough.

In a large bowl, use your hands to blend the flour and salt. Add the butter, then use your fingertips to mix the butter through the flour, separating the pieces and coating them with flour. *Keep the lumps intact.*

Sprinkle the cream over the mixture, never hitting the same place twice. Mix the dough with a few light strokes of the fork until it barely holds together—it will be infuriatingly crumbly. Let it rest in a cool place 15 minutes.

Now come the turns—the folding that captures air in the pastry and creates the layers. You'll make six turns in three steps. To keep track of the turns completed, press the same number of fingers into the dough, just as bakers do. The dough will be maddening to roll at first, but quickly becomes manageable.

The two turns: On a lightly floured kitchen towel or piece of canvas, roll out the dough ½

inch thick in a rectangle—6 by 9 inches is ideal. Whatever the size you make, keep it the same size each time you roll. Square the corners. On the long side, make a mark one-third in from the raggedyest end. Fold this end over the center third of the rectangle, then fold the other end over them both to make three equal layers. Give the dough a half turn so the side seams run perpendicular to the way they just were. Repeat the rolling and folding and turning one more time. Let the dough rest 30 minutes. If the room isn't cool, wrap the dough and put it in the vegetable crisper of the refrigerator.

Make the two turns two more times, allowing a rest of 30 minutes between them. On the final turn, flip the dough over so the bumpy side is up, and so when you make the last folds, the outside will be smooth. Wrap and put in the crisper for 30 minutes at least (or up to 24 hours) before rolling out for the tart pan. If it's cold, bring to cool room temperature before rolling out.

To continue, follow steps 8 through 10 on page 17. When you roll, try not to roll over the edges, which forces air out of the layers. Be sure to roll the dough wide enough so any excess falls over the outside of the rim, or it will shrink in baking and you'll have too shallow a shell for filling. Chill 1 hour before filling and baking or baking blind.

Skinny Pastry Made with Oil

This is melting-light pastry that's not only a breeze to put together, but has 40 percent less fat and 27 percent fewer calories than my short crust.

1 ⅔ cups bread flour or all-purpose flour
⅜ teaspoon baking powder (¼ plus ⅛ or
*   a rounded ¼ teaspoon)*
½ teaspoon sea salt
⅓ cup plus ½ tablespoon canola or other
*   mild-flavored oil, at room temperature*
Scant 3½ tablespoons tepid water

In a large bowl, use your hands to toss the flour, baking powder, and salt together until well mixed. Shake the oil and water in a jar until thoroughly blended. Continue by following steps 5 through 10 on page 17, using the hand mixing method. This dough doesn't always readily hold together, so just pat it firmly and patch when needed as you roll it out and fit it in the mold—and don't worry!

Crisp Sweet Pastry

This delectable pastry holds its texture under most fillings for 24 hours.

1⅔ cups bread flour or all-purpose flour
¼ cup sugar
⅜ teaspoon baking powder (¼ plus ⅛ or
*   a rounded ¼ teaspoon)*
¼ teaspoon sea salt
10 tablespoons (5 ounces) unsalted butter,
*   cool but supple*
1 large egg yolk
3 tablespoons cold heavy cream

Follow steps 1 through 6 on pages 16 and 17. Use the *fraisage* technique. Proceed by following steps 7 through 10 on page 17.

VARIATION: SPICED CRISP SWEET PASTRY

Just as herbs add a delicious dimension to savory flavors, spices add verve to sweet tastes. Add the spice(s) to the flour in Crisp Sweet Pastry—you can make a blend, just as you do in cakes and cookies. Of course, each spice has its affinities and, as with herbs, the amount to use depends on strength of flavor, the tart's filling, and the freshness and provenence of the spice. It's wise to add slowly and taste as you go along.

Here are a few classic affinities. Start with ½ tablespoon ground spice and taste from there. You may want the spice to be a murmur, you may want it to be the chorus.

allspice: nearly every fruit

anise seeds: creamy cheeses

cardamom: apples, almonds, oranges, pears, pistachios

cinnamon: all stone fruits, all pome fruits, most tropical fruits, all berries, chocolate, lemon, most nuts

cloves: nearly every fruit, especially oranges, pineapple

coriander: apples, lemons, oranges, tropical fruits, chocolate

ginger: all tropical fruits, chocolate

mace and nutmeg: nearly every fruit and creamy cheeses (mace is the warmer of the two)

Crunchy Graham-Pecan Crumb Crust

Easy, easy, easy. And scrumptious.

> 1 cup (about 2 ⅔ ounces) ground toasted pecans
> ½ tablespoon all-purpose flour
> 1 ounce bittersweet or semisweet chocolate
> 1¼ cups (16 to 17 squares) graham cracker crumbs
> ¼ cup sugar
> 6 tablespoons unsalted butter, melted

Use a food processor or blender to process the pecans with the flour until finely ground. To grate the chocolate, chop it into small pieces and pulse in a food processor until fairly finely grated, or use the medium-small blade of a hand grater.

Combine all ingredients except the butter in the food processor or mixing bowl and mix. Add the butter and blend thoroughly.

Press the mixture evenly into the mold ⅛ inch thick. Don't worry about it being all that even around the top —the filling will cover it. If you're making this with a ring, brace it against two sides of a rimmed baking sheet, or the ring will slide as you press and the crumbs with it.

Chill while heating the oven to 375°F. Bake until lightly browned, 10 to 11 minutes. Let cool in the mold on a rack. Leave it in the mold until the recipe tells you to unmold it.

European Hazelnut Pastry

You will end up with ample dough to make the base and lattice for one 11- to 11½-inch tart. This pastry is in the European tradition: short, lightly sweetened, superbly flavored, and just rich enough. What makes it so toothsome—barely enough moisture to hold everything together—makes it a little tricky to work. But be assured that the dough isn't harmed by working it, and although you have to patch the lattice strips like crazy, the patches hold beautifully in baking.

> 2¼ cups (generous 10 ounces) toasted,
>   unblanched hazelnuts or use almonds
> 1½ cups bread flour or all-purpose flour
> 6 tablespoons sugar
> Scant ½ teaspoon cinnamon
> Scant ¼ teaspoon ground cloves
> ¾ teaspoon unsweetened cocoa
> Zest of ½ large lemon
> 1 extra-large egg yolk, hard-cooked
> 12 tablespoons (6 ounces) unsalted butter,
>   cool but supple
> 2 large raw egg yolks

Combine the nuts and a small handful of the flour in a food processor. Pulse in short bursts just until the nuts are finely ground (you'll have a rounded 3 cups, lightly packed). Add the remaining flour, the sugar, cinnamon, cloves, cocoa, and lemon zest. Crumble in the hard-cooked yolk. Pulse until blended. Cut in the butter in thin ½-inch chips and pulse until the texture of cornmeal, about 24 times. Add the raw egg yolks and process until some of the dough comes together.

Turn out onto a big sheet of waxed paper. Knead until the crumbles hold together. If you're going mad because they won't, sprinkle over a *teaspoon* of ice water, then knead again. You can wrap and chill the dough for an hour or two or roll it out at once between sheets of waxed paper. If chilled until hard, bring to cool room temperature before rolling out. Roll out and bake according to the recipe.

After baking, this pastry is *very* fragile until it has thoroughly cooled, so don't disturb it. Set the baking sheet on a rack until cold, at which point it can be freed with a spatula and will easily come off the metal.

Toffee Crust

This yummy crust is just that—a bottom crust, rather than a shell. The composition is too ephemeral to stay up on the sides in baking: It's a little bit pastry, a little bit cookie, a little bit candy. The air beaten into the mixture makes it puff to a light and crunchy ⅜ inch high.

A toffee crust is good with any filling that doesn't need sides to hold it in place.

> Scant 1½ cups (4½ ounces) sliced
>   toasted almonds
> Scant 1½ tablespoons all-purpose flour
> 2 or 3 drops pure almond extract
> 8 tablespoons (4 ounces) unsalted butter,
>   softened to the consistency of mayonnaise
> ⅓ cup plus ¼ cup sugar

Heat the oven to 350°F. Combine the nuts and flour in a food processor or blender. Pulse or whirl in short bursts just until the nuts are finely ground. Add the remaining ingredients and process until fluffy.

Turn into the tart pan. Use a fork to smooth the mixture evenly over the bottom. Set on a pizza pan or baking sheet and bake until the color of toasted almonds, 12 to 15 minutes, but start checking after 10 minutes. Let cool in the pan on a rack. Compose the tart with or without the rim in place, but leave the base in place to serve.

MAKE-AHEAD NOTE: You can bake this crust a day in advance and keep it in a cool, dry place. Don't set anything juicy on top more than an hour before serving, but something that's firm and not moist can go on 4 to 5 hours ahead of time.

Meringue Shell

This is a delightfully Americanized version of classic Swiss *broyage*. Instead of meringue enriched with ground almonds and cornstarch, someone came up with the bright idea of using saltine crackers. Note that the mixing speeds are for a portable mixer; reduce the speed of a standard mixer by one notch.

4 extra-large egg whites, at room temperature
Pinch of salt
Scant ½ tablespoon baking powder
1¼ teaspoons pure vanilla extract
1⅓ cups sugar
*Rounded 3 tablespoons (5½ squares) finely
    rolled saltine crackers*

Heat the oven to 300°F. Line the bottom of the tart pan with brown paper (you can use the inside of a grocery bag), but do not butter it.

Place the egg whites and salt in a mixing bowl and beat on low speed until frothy. Add the baking powder and vanilla and beat on medium speed until soft peaks form. Increase the speed to high and very slowly beat in *⅔ cup of the sugar,* a tablespoon at a time. Beat another minute or two until very stiff and glossy. Combine the remaining sugar and the saltines and sprinkle over the mixture. Beat on low speed just until the sugar disappears.

Smooth the mixture into the pan. Bake until dry, 40 to 50 minutes. Remove to a rack out of a draft and let cool in the pan. The center will fall just enough to make room for the filling.

MAKE-AHEAD NOTE. Meringues can be baked 1 to 2 weeks in advance, as long as the air is dry; if it's damp, bake the shell no sooner than 12 hours ahead of time.

Recipes in this chapter:

43
NIÇOISE ZUCCHINI AND EGGPLANT TART
FOR BASTILLE DAY

*In a lean oil pastry shell, thin sautéed eggplant slices and two colors of zucchini are enriched
with garlic, thickly sauced with fresh tomatoes, and topped with Parmesan cheese
shavings, Niçoise olives, anchovies, fresh thyme, and red pepper flakes.*

45
TART OF BLACK BEANS, CORN, AND THREE COLORS OF SWEET PEPPERS
IN A BLUE CORNMEAL CRUST
FOR THE EARTH MOTHER

*Purply beans are slowly baked with garlic, then mashed and spread on a blue cornmeal crust.
Atop them are a pinwheel of grilled sweet pepper strips in red, green, and gold. Fresh
yellow corn kernels make a border, and perky cilantro sprigs fill the center.*

48
POTATO TART WITH GARLIC, HERBS, AND SMOKED SALMON
TO CELEBRATE FINNEGANS WAKE

*On a green bed of chopped parsley and green onions in a short crust shell, a buttery purée of yellow Irish
potatoes richly flavored with garlic is mantled with smoked salmon and garnished
with more green onions, parsley, and lemon wedges.*

50
A ROMAN WILD MUSHROOM TART
FOR SATURNALIA

*In a delectable shell of flaky pastry, fresh and dried wild mushrooms studded with red pearl onions are bound
with an herbal and lemony sauce and decorated with a nosegay of flat-leaf parsley.*

Tart of Hard-Cooked Eggs with Green Mayonnaise, Watercress, and Tulips

For Easter

The creamy gold that's usually plopped into the hollows of hard-cooked egg whites is the delectable filling of this tart. One ingredient makes it sublime—and you can keep it a secret. The mayonnaise, turned soft green with specks of watercress, also has a special element, but you'll recognize it on first bite. This is a marvelous way to begin a late breakfast, to nibble with drinks before a light supper, or to open any meal al fresco. For a festive Easter breakfast, you might offer a Gewürztraminer to sip with it.

MAKES 12 BUFFET OR APPETIZER SERVINGS

THE FILLING
13 eggs, hard-cooked and shelled
1 large green onion, white part only, cut up
½ cup plus 1 tablespoon best-quality mayonnaise
¼ cup plus ½ tablespoon Dijon mustard
4½ tablespoons (2¼ ounces) unsalted butter, melted and cooled
Sea salt and freshly ground white pepper, to taste

THE GREEN MAYONNAISE
1 cup best-quality mayonnaise

⅔ cup (about one 4-ounce bunch) firmly packed watercress leaves, rinsed and patted thoroughly dry
Rounded ½ teaspoon finely grated lemon zest
Sea salt and freshly ground white pepper, to taste
Fully baked Short Crust Pastry shell (page 22)
Sprigs and leaves from 1 bunch watercress, rinsed and patted thoroughly dry
1 big or several small unsprayed opened bright red, orange, or purple tulips
12 to 24 bright unsprayed tulip petals

33

To make the filling, neatly slice the eggs in half lengthwise. Turn the yolks into a food processor or blender. Wrap and refrigerate the 12 most handsome halves of whites. Add the rest to the yolks, along with the green onion, mayonnaise, and mustard. Process until smooth. With the motor running, drizzle in the butter. Taste for salt and pepper. Turn into a bowl, lay plastic wrap directly on the surface of the mixture, and refrigerate.

To make the mayonnaise, turn all ingredients except the salt and pepper into a food processor or blender. Pulse or whirl until well mixed. Taste for seasoning—salt will probably not be needed—then turn into a bowl. Cover and refrigerate at least 15 minutes to firm up. You will have 1 generous cup mayonnaise.

To compose the tart, set the shell on its serving platter. Spread the filling evenly over the bottom. Set the egg whites, flat sides down and evenly spaced, around the shell about 1 inch in from the rim—or wherever they'll fit fairly snugly—narrow ends pointing toward the center. Make a border of sprigs of watercress around the edge between the whites and the sides of the tart. Using a small spoon—or a decorating bag fitted with a star tip—drop a small flourish of green mayonnaise on each rounded egg (place it where you like). Tuck a watercress leaf into each flourish, then set a vibrant tulip (or several smaller ones) in the center of the tart.

To serve, cut into wedges so that each one is centered with a rounded egg white and its attendant watercress. Tuck 1 or 2 bright tulip petals (they're edible) at the top of the wedge in the cress.

MAKE-AHEAD NOTE: See make-ahead notes for pastries on page 19. The eggs can be hard-cooked a day before using, but don't shell them until a couple of hours before preparing. The filling can be prepared several hours in advance and kept covered in the refrigerator. The green mayonnaise can be prepared and refrigerated 1 day. Given a little time, the lemon zest kicks in and heightens the flavor all the more.

Springtime Tart of Scrambled Eggs

Warm a fully baked Short Herbal Pastry shell flavored with *fines herbes* (page 22). Fill with warm eggs softly scrambled with tender-cooked asparagus tips. Smooth the top, then arrange cooked asparagus spears on it, fanning them, tips out, from the center. Heap cooked asparagus tips in the center. Sprinkle the spears with a shredded mild cheese, drizzle the tart with nut-brown butter, and serve at once.

THYMED TARTLETS OF CARROTS

FOR THE WHITE RABBIT'S BIRTHDAY

Imagine the delight when your guests are served baby carrots nestled in a tartlet. The tartlets are fine companions for almost any simple dish of fish, fowl, or meat, and their vibrant color enhances the table. Or offer them as a first course, perhaps accompanied with a chilled dry sherry. If you can't buy packaged carrots trimmed to baby size, bring home the smallest, sweetest, tenderest carrots you can.

MAKES EIGHT 4-INCH TARTLETS

2 pounds tender, sweet tiny carrots,
    ideally 1 to 1¼ inches long by ¼ inch
    in diameter
Boiling water, as needed
Sea salt, to taste
12 tablespoons (6 ounces) unsalted butter,
    softened
About ¼ teaspoon ground dried thyme
About ½ teaspoon sugar
A little freshly ground white pepper
A good splash (about 4 teaspoons) brandy
8 fully baked Short Crust Pastry 4-inch
    tartlet shells (page 22)
¼ cup chopped fresh chervil or flat-leaf parsley

If the carrots are unpeeled, simply scrub them. For the star on top of the tartlets, select the handsomest 40 carrots of uniform size. If you don't have tiny carrots, trim the bottoms of 40 small carrots to form them. Or simply cut young carrots into 40 matchsticks of the same size. Set them aside. Turn the remaining carrots into a large, heavy skillet and add boiling water to cover. Add salt and cook briskly uncovered until thoroughly tender when pierced with a thin skewer, 10 to 12 minutes.

Scoop out the carrots with a slotted spoon (leave the water) and pass them through the medium blade of a food mill or mash them well

with a fork. Blend in 8 tablespoons (yes!) of the butter and the thyme, sugar, and pepper to taste. Cover loosely and set aside.

Turn the 40 carrots and the remaining 4 tablespoons butter into the water in the skillet and cook as before just until tender-crisp, about 10 minutes. Add water if needed to prevent scorching, but allow the liquid to reduce to nothing toward the end so the carrots are glazed in the butter. When the carrots are ready, sprinkle them with the brandy and shake the carrots back and forth until each has its nip of spirits. Remove from the heat and cover loosely.

To serve, heat the oven to 375°F. Set the tartlet shells on a baking sheet. Divide the purée among them, then gently smooth it over the bottom of each shell. Make a star of 5 carrots (or matchsticks) on top of each tartlet. Lay a sheet of aluminum foil over the tartlets, shiny side down. Bake until hot (to test, quickly dip a fingertip in the purée), about 25 minutes.

Dust the purée with a little lacy chervil or parsley, setting each star of carrots in relief. Serve at once on paper doily–lined small warmed plates.

MAKE-AHEAD NOTE: See make-ahead notes for pastries on page 19. Both the puréed and glazed carrots can be prepared several hours in advance.

Minty Tartlets of Garden Peas

Simmer shelled fresh garden peas with some of their pods and a few green onions until tender. Purée and lighten with butter and cream. Half-fill fully baked tartlet shells of Short Crust Pastry (page 22) with the purée, sprinkle with minced fresh mint, and then fill to the brim with tender-cooked garden peas. Dot with unsalted butter, grind over pepper, and lay a sheet of aluminum foil over the tartlets, shiny side down. Bake in a 375°F oven until hot. Serve hot with small mint leaves strewn on top.

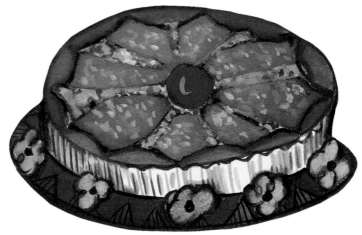

CREAMY FINES HERBES QUICHE

The bouquet of flat-leaf parsley, tarragon, chervil, and chives in this tart is a classic French seasoning for eggs. Chervil is a small lacy leaf that hints of anise. It's one of the easiest herbs to grow, but is inexplicably rare in our markets. Dried chervil leaves aren't worth eating, so if you can't find fresh leaves, substitute fennel leaves or increase the other herbs. Dried tarragon leaves do have true tarragon flavor, so use them if fresh are unavailable. The filling in this tart is light light light and creamy. Parmesan in the crust is another reason this tart is luxe. I roll the dough thicker for a quiche because it gives greater insurance against leaks in baking, gives more support to the fragile filling when unmolding it, guarantees the crust won't get soggy, and gives crunchy contrast to the velvety cream. This is a special-occasion dish filled to the brim with special-occasion ingredients (akin to lobster Newburg, but easier on the purse). If your circle is forever on a diet, rather than not eat this tart, make it with low-fat ingredients. I've included the alternatives in parentheses

in the recipe. Just use natural ingredients—nothing labeled "light" that contains fillers. They're ruinous when cooked. Make this extraordinary tart as the centerpiece for a celebratory feast. Accompany it with a colorful salad of red-leaf and romaine lettuces and the bitter leaves of escarole, curly chicory, radicchio, Belgian endive, dandelion—dressed with walnut or hazelnut oil and red wine vinegar. Drink champagne, and for dessert, swirl together raspberry, orange, and lemon ices and sauce them with crushed sweetened strawberries.

MAKES 8 TO 10 SERVINGS

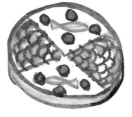

THE FINES HERBES

¼ cup finely snipped fresh or
  1 tablespoon plus ½ teaspoon crumbled
  dried tarragon leaves
¼ cup finely snipped fresh flat-leaf parsley
  leaves or a little more curly-leaf parsley
¼ cup finely snipped fresh chives leaves or
  shallot or green onion leaves
Rounded ¼ cup finely snipped fresh chervil
  leaves or a scant ¼ cup finely
  snipped fennel leaves

8 ounces cream cheese (Neufchâtel),
  at room temperature
1 cup heavy cream (milk)
⅓ cup sour cream (low-fat plain yogurt)
4 large eggs
2 large egg yolks (1 egg white)
Scant ½ teaspoon sea salt
Freshly ground white pepper, to taste
Fully baked Short Parmesan Pastry shell
  (page 22) in its mold
About 1 tablespoon Dijon mustard
Rounded ¼ cup coarsely snipped fresh
  fines herbes, for garnish
Sprigs of tarragon, flat-leaf parsley,
  and chervil and short bunches of chives for
  decorating the platter

Have all the ingredients at room temperature. Prepare the *fines herbes.* The reason you should snip herbs with scissors into a measuring cup rather than chop them on a board or in a machine is so no essence nor bit of leaf is wasted.

If you're using dried tarragon and baking the custard straightaway, the first thing to do is blend the dried leaves into a little of the cream, bring to a simmer, and steep until needed.

As you make the filling, mix only as much as is necessary to blend the ingredients fully. Air beaten into the custard makes it rise, but then it collapses on cooling, and the texture suffers. Air also increases the volume, and the filling might not fit into the shell.

In a food processor or with a mixer set on the lowest workable speed, pulse or beat the cream cheese until smooth. With the motor or beaters running, add the cream, sour cream, whole eggs, and egg yolks, pulsing or beating just until smooth after each addition. Blend in the *fines herbes* (including the cream if used for steeping the dried tarragon), and then the salt and pepper.

To bake, heat the oven to 350°F. Set the shell on a pizza pan or baking sheet. Brush the bottom with a veil of mustard. When the oven is ready, stir the custard briefly to mix it, then pour it into the shell. Use a spoon to distribute the herbs evenly in the custard. Bake until a knife comes out clean when inserted about 2 inches away from the center, 25 to 28 minutes. The custard will continue baking out of the oven.

Unmold and slide the tart onto its serving platter. Strew the top with the coarsely snipped *fines herbes,* and then decorate the platter with the herb sprigs and bunches. Serve hot or warm.

MAKE-AHEAD NOTE: See make-ahead notes for pastries on page 19. The custard preparation can be mixed an hour or two in advance. For matchless quality, serve the quiche hot or warm—within an hour or two of baking.

Swiss Cheese Soufflé Tart

Return a fully baked Short Parmesan Pastry shell (page 22) to its mold. Sprinkle the bottom with caraway seeds, then smooth in a 6-egg soufflé preparation flavored with Swiss cheese and a little crumbled crisp bacon. Run a finger around inside the rim (this will give the soufflé a hat). Sprinkle with grated Parmesan cheese and bake in a 400°F oven until puffed but still moist, about 15 minutes. Lift off the ring and serve at once on its base on a hot platter bordered with buttery chopped cooked spinach.

Bouquet of Vegetables Tart

In Honor of Thomas Jefferson's Monticello Garden

The muted colors and pure flavors of this tart are a celebration of vegetables. Rosy ham beneath the vegetables makes a serving a meal. If you prefer to omit the ham, increase the amount of each vegetable a little, and you'll have a lean tart. Serve with a salad of curly endive barely dressed with lemon juice and light-tasting olive oil. The ideal wine for the hues and flavors of this tart is a dry rosé. For dessert, purple plum crisp. Preparations for this tart take a bit of time, since each vegetable must be cooked separately. But there's nothing complicated about any of the steps—and the tart is so beautiful, it's time happily spent. Everything goes much faster than the reading implies. If you can't buy carrots trimmed to baby size, cut young tender ones into matchsticks of the size described.

MAKES 8 SERVINGS

Short Herbal Pastry dough flavored with
    rosemary (page 22)
8 ounces lean, skinless ham, sliced ¼ inch thick
8 uniform cherry tomatoes, each 1 inch
    in diameter
1 large (8 ounces) zucchini, trimmed
3 large leeks, white part only
2¼ cups (10 ounces) baby carrots, all 1 to 1¼
    inches long by ¼ inch wide
3 cups water
½ teaspoon sea salt, plus more to taste
1 tablespoon mild-flavored oil
8 uniform mushroom caps, all 2 inches
    in diameter
2 tablespoons unsalted butter, softened, plus a
    little more that has been melted
Freshly ground white pepper, to taste

THE CUSTARD

4 large eggs, at room temperature
1 cup half-and-half or milk, at room temperature
Heaped 1 tablespoon finely shredded lemon zest

A nosegay of unsprayed coppery nasturtiums or
    other rose-gold flowers or a bunch of flat-leaf
    parsley

Roll out the dough as described on page 14. Then, following the direction on page 15 for making a decorative border, trim the dough to leave a ½-inch overhang. Fold it down inside so the sides stand 1¼ inches high. Flute the edge, making sure no fluting sticks out past the rim; if it does, it will break off when you remove the ring. Bake as for a custard filling as directed on page 39. Let cool.

Cut the ham slices into pieces ½ inch long and set aside. As you prepare each vegetable for cooking, cover it and keep it cool; do the same after they've been cooked. Drop the tomatoes into a medium-sized pot of boiling water, count 30 seconds, and then lift out and peel. Set on a dish.

Slice the zucchini ¼ inch thick on the diagonal. Stack the slices, and again slice on the diagonal to make ¼-inch-wide matchsticks with green tips at either end; you will have about 1⅓ cups. Slice the leeks crosswise ¼ inch thick. As you work with the leek slices, try to keep them intact as much as possible, rather than ending up with a jillion rings. Place the slices in a strainer and gently rinse them under running water to remove any soil trapped in their layers.

Scrub the carrots, if unpeeled. Have ready a big bowl of ice water. Bring the 3 cups water and ½ teaspoon salt to a boil in a large heavy skillet. Drop in the carrots and boil uncovered until *almost* tender when pierced with a thin skewer, 5 to 8 minutes, but start checking after a few minutes. Lift out with a slotted spoon—leave the

water—and drop the carrots into the ice water to stop the cooking. When cool, scoop them out with the slotted spoon onto a folded kitchen towel to dry. Add ice to the bowl of water.

Return the carrot water to a boil and drop in the zucchini. Cook uncovered, stirring, until the pieces are barely tender, 2 to 3 minutes after the water has returned to a boil. Lift out and drop into the ice water. When they're cool, drain and spread them out on a folded kitchen towel.

Turn the cooking liquid into something to save it. Dry the skillet, add the oil, and heat it over medium heat. Add the leeks and cook gently, stirring occasionally, until lightly browned on both sides, about 2 minutes. Add the saved liquid and simmer until the leeks are tender, about 3 minutes more. Lift them out with the slotted spoon onto toweling as well.

If you have a canelle knife and if you feel like it, flute the mushroom caps in 5 or 6 swirls from the center. Add 1 tablespoon of the butter to the stock in the skillet, add the mushrooms and shake and turn over medium heat until they're glazed all over—you may have to add a bit of water—4 to 5 minutes. Remove them, top sides up, to a dish.

To bake, heat the oven to 375°F. Set the tart shell on a pizza pan or rimmed baking sheet. Brush the bottom with the remaining 1 table-spoon softened butter. Strew the ham evenly over the bottom. Fit the tomatoes shoulder to shoulder in a ring at the center. Make a ring of leeks around them (toward the edge). Next fit the car-rots in a ring outside the leeks—leaving room for a border of the zucchini, which you'll place last. Each vegetable should be given roughly an equal width of space—although the carrots will domi-nate, the green tips of the zucchini are as impor-tant to the finished composition. Sprinkle with salt and pepper.

To make the custard, break the eggs into a measuring jug and add the half-and-half or milk to the 2-cup mark, and lemon zest, and beat with a fork just until blended (don't beat in additional air). Pour over the tart, then shake the tart to set-tle the mixture.

Bake until a table knife inserted where the leeks are comes out clean; start testing after 50 minutes. The custard will still appear to be wet in places, but it will be set underneath.

About 5 minutes before serving, toss the mushrooms in a dry skillet to warm them up. Set a mushroom on a line with a cherry tomato. With a soft brush, quickly baste the vegetables with a little melted butter to make them glisten. Slide onto its platter and serve hot or warm with a nosegay of flowers or parsley in the center.

MAKE-AHEAD NOTE: See make-ahead notes for pastries on page 19. The ham and vegetables can be cut up several hours in advance. The vegeta-bles can be cooked a couple of hours before they go into the tart.

NIÇOISE ZUCCHINI AND EGGPLANT TART

FOR BASTILLE DAY

In the heat of summer, a fresh way with zucchini is always welcome. This calls for both green and golden zucchini. Two colors are handsome but not crucial to the success of the tart. If you have an abundance of zucchini in one color, use it. Serve with grilled chicken and a sprightly red wine—perhaps a Côtes-du-Rhône. No need for cheese to follow, but a salad of bitter greens is ideal. For dessert, slice peeled ripe peaches into goblets, sprinkle with sugar, and splash with some of the same wine.

MAKES 8 SERVINGS

1 medium-large (12 ounces) purple eggplant, unpeeled, cut crosswise into ¼-inch-thick slices, and the slices quartered

1 teaspoon sea salt, plus more to taste

2½ tablespoons olive oil, plus more to finish

1 medium-large yellow onion, finely chopped

10 medium-large (generous 1¼ pounds) ripe plum tomatoes, coarsely chopped

Freshly ground white pepper, to taste

2 medium-large (12 ounces) yellow zucchini, sliced ⅜ inch thick

2 medium-large (12 ounces) green zucchini, sliced ⅜ inch thick

1 whole head garlic, chopped (scant ¼ cup)

½ to 1 cup (¾ to 1½ ounces) Parmesan cheese shavings, according to taste

1 tablespoon fresh or 1 teaspoon crumbled dried thyme leaves

1 teaspoon red pepper flakes, or to taste

One 2-ounce can flat anchovy fillets, drained

24 salt-cured olives

Fully baked Skinny Pastry Made with Oil shell—use a mild tasting olive oil (page 24)

Usually I don't salt eggplant—a common European practice—but for dishes like this, salt extracts juices from eggplant flesh. As a result, you need only a soupçon of fat for cooking it, and the flavor is more concentrated.

Turn the eggplant into a colander and sprinkle with the 1 teaspoon salt. Let drain 30 to 60 minutes, mixing with your hands occasionally, while continuing.

Heat 1 tablespoon of the oil in a heavy, medium-sized skillet over medium-high heat. Add the onion and sauté, stirring frequently, until translucent, about 2 minutes. Add the tomatoes and a little salt and pepper, and cook, stirring frequently, until reduced to a generous 1¼ cups of thick sauce, about 8 minutes. Taste for seasoning, then cover and set aside.

Heat ½ tablespoon of the oil in a large, heavy skillet over medium-high heat. Add the yellow and green zucchini, sprinkle with salt and pepper, and sauté, stirring frequently with a wooden spoon, until almost tender, about 3 minutes. Turn into a large bowl and cover. Do not rinse the skillet.

Squeeze the juice from the eggplant and pat the pieces dry with toweling. Meanwhile, heat the remaining 1 tablespoon oil in the skillet over medium-high heat. Add the eggplant and sauté, stirring frequently, until tender and nicely browned, 12 to 15 minutes. Add to the zucchini. Again, there is no need to rinse the skillet.

Return the dry skillet to a burner over medium-high heat. When hot, add the garlic and cook, stirring constantly, until it starts to color, about 1 minute. Remove from the heat, add the zucchini and eggplant, and mix well.

To serve, heat the oven to 400°F. Smooth the eggplant mixture into the shell. Set the shell on a pizza pan or baking sheet. Spread the tomato sauce evenly over the surface, top with the cheese shavings, and then sprinkle with the thyme and red pepper flakes. Arrange the anchovy fillets in a spoke pattern on top. Bake about 15 minutes. Remove from the oven and set 3 olives at the rim end of each anchovy. Return to the oven and bake until hot (to test, quickly dip a fingertip near the center), about 25 minutes in all.

Slide the tart onto a heated platter, drizzle with a thread of oil for highlights, and serve at once, cutting into wedges so that there is a strip of anchovy down the center of each slice.

MAKE-AHEAD NOTE: See make-ahead notes for pastries on page 19. The filling elements can be prepared several hours in advance, covered, and refrigerated, then brought to room temperature before combining in the shell for baking.

Tart of Black Beans, Corn, and Three Colors of Sweet Peppers in a Blue Cornmeal Crust

FOR THE EARTH MOTHER

Inspired by the colors and flavors of the old Southwest, this is a wonderfully satisfying tart, yet lean and easy to put together. It's a complete vegetarian meal, or you can offer grilled chicken on the side. Drink cold beer, have a bowl of green and black olives and radishes on the table, follow with crackers and a fresh creamy cheese mixed with herbs, and then for dessert, grapefruit ice. (To make this coarse and refreshing ice, combine puréed grapefruit flesh and simmered-until-tender finely shredded grapefruit zest in proportions you like, sweeten to taste, and freeze in a pan, stirring occasionally. Serve when it's an icy slush, topped with fresh mint.) The beans are so delicious, you'd be wise to double the ingredients given, and cook a pound of them, eating the leftovers a day or two later. You'll find the baking technique is the best—the enlightened—way to cook them.

MAKES 8 SERVINGS

THE BEANS

1⅓ cups (8 ounces) black beans, rinsed and
* picked over*

2 or 3 large garlic cloves

½ teaspoon sea salt, or to taste

Boiling water, as needed

1 tablespoon fresh lemon juice

4 fresh red or green jalapeño chilies, or to taste,
* quartered lengthwise, and seeds removed,*
* if desired*

3 large sweet peppers, 1 red, 1 yellow,
* and 1 green, each 8 ounces and 5 to 6 inches*
* long, quartered lengthwise and seeds removed*

1½ cups (from 2 large ears) freshly cut yellow
* corn kernels*

¾ cup milk (nonfat is fine)

Sea salt and freshly ground black pepper, to taste

Partially baked (until the rim is pale brown)
* Cornmeal Pastry shell made with dried blue*
* corn kernels (page 23)*

⅓ cup chopped cilantro

Small nosegay of cilantro sprigs

To prepare the beans, heat the oven to 250°F. Turn the beans and garlic cloves into an oven-proof pot (preferably earthenware) with the salt. Add boiling water to cover by 3 inches. Cover and bake until tender, about 3 hours. Check the water level every half hour or so, and add boiling water as needed to keep the beans covered. Stir occasionally. Drain, saving the stock. You'll have about 3 cups (garlic included). Mash the beans with a fork, leaving some whole for texture. Add about ½ cup of the bean stock to make a moist mash. Stir in the lemon juice, cover, and set aside.

Heat 2 large dry cast-iron and/or heavy non-stick skillets over high heat. Add the chilies and sweet peppers, skin sides down. Cover and pan roast, turning frequently with tongs, until tender. Start checking the chilies after about 8 minutes. At once turn the tender pieces into a paper bag and close the top—steam will help loosen the skin. When cool enough to handle, peel the pieces. I like to leave a little skin on for gloss and flavor. Cut the sweet peppers lengthwise into strips 1 inch wide. Finely chop the chilies and blend into the beans. Taste for salt.

To serve, heat the oven to 400°F. Spread the beans evenly in the tart shell in its mold. Lay the sweet pepper strips flat over the surface, fanning them out from the center and alternating the red, yellow, and green. Toward the center, the strips will be heaped. Rest a sheet of aluminum foil on top, shiny side down, and bake until the beans are hot (to test, quickly dip a fingertip in the center), about 20 minutes.

While the tart bakes, combine the corn and the milk in a small pan and simmer until the corn is tender, 3 to 5 minutes. Taste for salt and pepper. Use a slotted spoon to spoon the hot corn around the tart's edge in a border about 1½ inches wide. Unmold and slide onto a hot platter. Sprinkle chopped cilantro over the corn, then set the cilantro nosegay in the center. Serve at once.

MAKE-AHEAD NOTE: See make-ahead notes for pastries on page 19. The beans can be cooked a couple of days in advance. The sweet and chili peppers can be prepared several hours ahead of time. If the beans and peppers are refrigerated, bring to room temperature before composing the tart.

Punjabi Curried Red Bean Tart

Bake dried red beans with a bay leaf according to the black bean recipe (page 46). Lift out the beans with a slotted spoon (save the stock) and mash half of them with a fork. In a skillet, heat a little oil over medium heat. When hot, add as much minced fresh ginger, garlic, and curry powder as you'd like and stir for 1 to 2 minutes. Blend in all the beans, moisten with bean stock, and brighten with fresh lime juice and ground coriander. Heat until piping hot, stirring occasionally, then smooth into a heated fully baked Short Wheaten Pastry shell (page 22). Cover thickly with cool diced tomatoes mixed with chopped green onions and purple-leaf basil, drizzle with mild oil, and garnish with cilantro sprigs. Serve with chutney and a yogurt-and-cucumber salad.

POTATO TART WITH GARLIC, HERBS, AND SMOKED SALMON

Here's heaven for potato lovers. Serve this rich but light tart with mugs of Guinness stout and a crisp green salad. Follow with wheat crackers and a sharp cheese. For dessert, pass a basket of strawberries or cherries or plums or apples—the best the season has to offer. To make this on the spur of the moment when good smoked salmon isn't in the house, finish the tart with thin slices of cool tomatoes just before serving.

MAKES 8 SERVINGS

THE POTATOES
6 to 7 medium-sized (2½ pounds) yellow potatoes,
  peeled and cut into smallish chunks
3½ heads (8 ounces) garlic, unpeeled,
  separated into cloves
Sea salt, to taste
Overflowing ½ cup sour cream
3 ounces cream cheese, softened
Freshly ground white pepper, to taste

Unbaked Short Crust Pastry shell (page 22)
2 tablespoons Dijon mustard
½ cup chopped green onions, including leaves
½ cup chopped fresh parsley, preferably curly
1½ tablespoons unsalted butter, melted
10 ounces very thinly sliced smoked salmon
8 lemon wedges
Big parsley sprig for garnish

Steam or boil the potatoes until tender, about 25 minutes. Meanwhile, in a small covered pan, simmer the garlic cloves in an inch of lightly salted water until tender, about 30 minutes. Drain, then peel the garlic by pulling off the skin from the top end. Pop out the clove.

Purée the potatoes and garlic together through a food mill or ricer or mash with a potato masher (no lumps). Blend in the sour cream and cream cheese, then add salt and pepper.

To bake, heat the oven to 400°F. Set the tart shell on a pizza pan or baking sheet. Brush the bottom with the mustard. Mix the green onions and chopped parsley together, then sprinkle the bottom evenly with ½ cup of the mixture. Smooth in the purée and drizzle with the melted butter.

Bake until the pastry is golden and the potatoes are piping hot (to test, quickly dip a fingertip in the center to see), about 40 minutes. Check after about 25 minutes. If the potatoes are browning too fast, lay a sheet of aluminum foil on top, shiny side down. Remove from the oven and immediately cover the top with the salmon, fanning large slices out from the center and filling the spaces with smaller pieces. Unmold and slide onto 2 hot platters.

To serve, sprinkle the rest of the green onion mixture around the rim of the tart. Make a star of the lemon wedges in the center, and set a furl of parsley in the middle of the star. Serve at once, cutting each slice to include a wedge of lemon for squirting over the salmon. Lemon and potato are marvelous together.

MAKE-AHEAD NOTE: See make-ahead notes for pastries on page 19. The purée can be prepared and refrigerated a day before baking, but bring it to room temperature before turning it into the shell.

Roasted Garlic Tartlets

Heap fully baked tiny tartlet shells of sage-flavored Short Herbal Pastry (page 22) with peeled roasted garlic cloves. Drizzle with fruity olive oil and sprinkle with tiny dice of pimiento, wisps of lemon zest, and minced parsley. Serve cool with sprigs of parsley on the side for the timid to chew.

A Roman Wild Mushroom Tart

For Saturnalia

An ancient Roman festival still held in parts of Britain around December 17, Saturnalia celebrates the arrival of the winter solstice with feasting and revelry. And what better feasting and reveling than in the treasures of the forest floor? I read with envy of markets in autumn brimming with baskets of chanterelles, boletes (aka porcini and cèpes), horns of plenty, matsutake, and hedgehog mushrooms. If you, like me, aren't so lucky—or if wild mushrooms are a fortune and your mushroom-gathering knowhow is rusty—buy what wild ones you can, and let common cultivated mushrooms make up the rest of the filling. They'll absorb the flavor of the richer mushrooms. You can do Deborah Madison's trick of cutting the old familiar mushrooms into irregular pieces to give them chunkiness and mystery ("The Greens Cookbook"). A balanced mix of fresh and dried mushrooms gives depth of flavor, but you've got to know your flavors to put them together, lest a strong mushroom overwhelms delicate ones. I've found dried morels and fresh shiitakes with cultivated mushrooms

wonderful—fresh chanterelles and dried porcini are special together, too. I like to include dark-capped mushrooms in the composition, if only a handful. They add as much beauty as the lavender of the pearl onions and the green of the parsley.

Serve this rapturous tart as a main dish for luncheon, drinking a lightly chilled Valpolicella. To complement—not compete with—the complex flavors of the mushrooms, salad should be just butter lettuces with lemon juice and walnut oil. After, offer an assortment of Italian cheeses with crackers. For dessert, I make a bittersweet chocolate soufflé in a shallow gratin dish, the bottom spread with tart cherry preserves.

MAKES 8 SERVINGS

1⅓ cups (1 ounce) dried whole or pieces of morels
    or porcini or other richly flavored
    wild mushrooms
2 cups good lightly salted chicken broth
2 cups (10 ounces) red pearl onions or 1-inch
    chunks of larger red onions
2 large (8 ounces) fresh shiitake or other
    delicate mushrooms
1 pound fresh cultivated button mushrooms,
    each 1 to 1¼ inches in diameter
Fully baked Flaky Pastry shell (page 23)
4 tablespoons extra-virgin olive oil
2½ teaspoons (about 3 cloves) finely chopped garlic
2 tablespoons all-purpose flour
3 to 4 tablespoons fresh lemon juice
2 egg yolks
Freshly ground black pepper and sea salt, to taste
½ cup (firmly packed) chopped flat-leaf parsley
Small bouquet of flat-leaf parsley sprigs

Swish the dried mushrooms briefly in a bowl of cool water to rinse them. Drain and turn them into a quart-sized bowl with the chicken broth. Steep for at least 1 hour—or up to 2 or 3 hours. When they're plump and tender, lift out the mushrooms, squeezing their liquid back into the bowl. Pass the steeping liquid through a damp cloth into a bowl. Slice plumped mushrooms into large-bite size, making shapes as different as possible. There will be about 1½ cups.

To blanch and peel the pearl onions, bring a pan of lightly salted water to a boil and drop them in. Boil, uncovered, 3 minutes. Drain and immerse in cold water. Using scissors, snip off the onions' roots and wispy tags. Peel the onions and keep them in a bowl. If you're using small chunks of red onions, simmer them very gently in lightly salted water until tender-crisp, taking care to keep the pieces together as much as possible. Remove from the heat and leave in the skillet.

Use a stainless steel knife to prepare the fresh mushrooms. Trim off any tough stems (they can be used for making broth for another dish). Cut the caps crosswise into ¼-inch-thick slices. Cut the cultivated mushrooms in thirds or halves lengthwise, starting the knife anywhere in the cap and cutting randomly, so that the chunks are refreshingly irregular.

To serve, set the tart shell on a heatproof platter. Place in the oven on its lowest setting to warm the shell. Using 1 large and 1 medium-sized nonreactive or nonstick skillet, heat 1 tablespoon of the olive oil in the smaller pan, and 2 tablespoons of the oil in the larger pan. Add the pearl onions to the smaller pan and turn the heat to low. Add the shiitakes or their equivalent to the larger pan.

After a minute or so, add the reconstituted mushrooms to the pearl onions. After about 3 minutes, add the fresh cultivated mushrooms and another tablespoon of oil to the shiitakes—they will have soaked up all the oil. Set the timer for 6 minutes. Shake both skillets frequently.

When the timer rings, turn the heat to low under the shiitakes and stir in the garlic. Sauté about 2 minutes, stirring frequently, then blend in the reconstituted mushrooms and pearl onions. Sprinkle the flour over the surface and stir it in with a wooden spoon. When it has been absorbed, after about 1 minute, blend in ½ cup of the reserved steeping broth, then 3 tablespoons of the lemon juice. Raise the heat to medium and stir until thickened, about 1 minute.

If you're using them, heat the small chunks of red onion in their pan.

In a small bowl, use a fork to blend another ½ cup of the steeping broth with the egg yolks. Stir it into the pan with the mushrooms. Raise the heat to medium-high and stir until everything is well mixed and the sauce is thickened. Grind over the pepper, taste for salt and tartness—do you want that last tablespoon of lemon juice?—then blend in the parsley. Cook 30 seconds, then turn into the tart shell, gently spooning in the onion chunks, if used, setting them here and there. Set the bouquet of parsley in the center and serve at once.

MAKE-AHEAD NOTE: See make-ahead notes for pastries on page 19. The dried mushrooms can be reconstituted and sliced and the pearl onions blanched and peeled several hours before composing the tart. A long hour before baking, the fresh mushrooms can be sliced, the lemon juice reamed, and the garlic and parsley chopped. Cover all ingredients except the tart shell with plastic wrap.

Tart of Braised Florence Fennel on a Bed of Golden Couscous

Sauté instant couscous in unsalted butter with sliced almonds and a little turmeric until you can smell the spice. Add a pinch of cinnamon and cook as directed on the package. Meanwhile, thinly slice tender bulbs of Florence fennel. Heat a splash of olive oil in a skillet. Add the fennel and sauté, stirring until you can smell it. Pour in chicken broth to barely cover, squeeze more lemon juice, and simmer, covered, until tender. Fill a fully baked Short Wheaten Pastry shell (page 22) with the couscous. Arrange the fennel on top. Strew with large dark raisins, drizzle with olive oil, lay aluminum foil, shiny side down, lightly on top, and bake until hot. Serve mantled with finely chopped raw red onion, cilantro, and flat-leaf parsley.

A Shrimp Feast of a Tart, New Orleans Style

To Honor Louis "Satchmo" Armstrong

An extravagance of three sizes of rosy shrimps in a sensationally flavored sauce of savory vegetables, this is the perfect tart for a gala occasion. The tricky part is finding good bay shrimps. I'm grateful to have discovered Pandalus shrimps from Oregon. They're larger than the puny babies usually available at the market, and tasty. If you can't find their equal, substitute the smallest available raw shrimps. This tart takes a bit of doing, but you'll be pleased with the results. A watercress salad and a crisp, dry Sauvignon Blanc are all you need for accompaniment. Perhaps a fresh cream cheese and crackers to refresh the palate afterward. For dessert, serve lemon sherbet sprinkled with shreds of orange zest and orange-flavored liqueur.

MAKES 8 SERVINGS

2 pounds cooked bay shrimps, thawed, if frozen

32 to 34 pieces (1 pound) raw medium-large
 shrimps

9 pieces (generous 8 ounces) raw large shrimps

THE STOCK

8 cups water

2½ teaspoons sea salt

Rounded ½ tablespoon cayenne pepper

Rounded ½ tablespoon celery seeds

Rounded ½ tablespoon ground coriander

Rounded ½ tablespoon dried dill

Rounded ½ tablespoon dry mustard

Scant 1 teaspoon ground cloves

5 large fresh bay leaves or 2 small dried bay leaves,
 torn into small pieces

THE SAUCE

3 tablespoons unsalted butter

3 medium-small ripe plum tomatoes, cut into
 ½-inch dice (1¼ cups)

1 large red onion, cut into ½-inch dice (1 cup)

2 celery ribs, cut into ¼-inch dice (1 cup)

1 small yellow sweet pepper, cut into ½-inch
 dice (½ cup)

1 small green sweet pepper, cut into ½-inch
 dice (½ cup)

2 fresh jalapeño chilies, seeds removed
 and thinly sliced (¼ cup)

3 large garlic cloves, thinly sliced

3 tablespoons plus 1 teaspoon cornstarch

Sea salt, to taste

Fully baked Short Crust Pastry shell (page 22)

2½ cups cider vinegar

1 cup dry white wine

Rounded 2½ teaspoons ground thyme

9 leafy flat-leaf parsley sprigs

If the bay shrimps have been thawed, turn them into a large sieve to drain thoroughly. Peel the raw shrimps, discarding the tails of the medium-sized shrimps, but leaving the tails on the big guys. Turn the shrimp shells into a large heavy pot. Devein the shrimps, if they need it. Refrigerate separately.

To make the stock, add the water, salt, cayenne, celery seeds, coriander, dill, mustard, cloves, and bay to the shells. Bring to a boil, turn the heat to low, and simmer uncovered for 1 hour. Pass the stock through a sieve, rinse the pot, then return the stock to the pot. Place over high heat, bring to a boil, and boil until reduced to 3⅓ cups. Remove a ladleful to a bowl and put the bowl in the freezer to cool quickly.

To make the sauce, melt the butter in a large, heavy nonstick skillet over high heat. Add all of the vegetables except the garlic and sauté, stirring frequently, until the onion, celery, and peppers are tender-crisp, 3 to 4 minutes. Stir in the garlic and turn off the heat.

Sprinkle the cornstarch into the cooled ladleful of stock and whisk until smooth. Whisk this mixture back into the vegetables, then continue to whisk while slowly adding the rest of the stock. When smooth, turn the heat to medium-high,

and whisk while the sauce thickens, about 1 minute. Turn the heat to medium and simmer for 2 minutes, stirring once or twice. Taste for salt.

To serve, slide the shell onto a heatproof platter. Place in the oven on its lowest setting to warm the shell. Reheat the sauce gently in a covered saucepan over low heat. Do not let it boil.

Turn the bay shrimps into a medium-sized, heavy-bottomed nonreactive skillet. Blend the vinegar, wine, and thyme in a large nonreactive skillet and bring to a boil over high heat. Pour just enough of this marinade over the bay shrimps to cover them, place on the stove, clap on a lid, and turn the heat to its lowest.

To cook the raw shrimps, return the marinade to a boil, drop in the jumbo shrimps, cover, and shake the skillet for 30 seconds. Add the medium-sized shrimps and repeat. Immediately turn off the heat and keep covered until all the shrimps have turned pink and are hot when you test them with a fingertip. Quickly drain all the shrimps into a large sieve, shaking off the marinade. Pull out the large shrimps.

Arrange the bay and medium-sized shrimps in the tart shell and spoon over an ample amount of the sauce, turning the rest into a heated bowl. Quickly arrange 8 large shrimps in a pinwheel over the center, then set the ninth shrimp in the center. Tuck a furl of parsley at the tip of each tail, and rush to the table.

MAKE-AHEAD NOTE: See make-ahead notes for pastries on page 19. The sauce can be completely prepared and the shrimps can be peeled and deveined in the morning. Refrigerate them both, then bring to room temperature before continuing.

Pernod Shrimp Tart

Stir an abundance of raw medium-sized shrimps (peeled and deveined, but their tails left on) with chopped shallots over high heat in half olive oil, half butter just until coral. Turn into a hot fully baked Short Crust Pastry shell (page 22). Flavor thick hot cream sauce with Pernod and pour over the shrimps. Shake gently to settle the sauce. Sprinkle with nutmeg and serve hot with braised baby artichokes on the side.

Seafood Tart Provençal

To Celebrate Life in the South of France

I wanted a lusty vivid tart heaped with seafood, and this is it. The flavors and sauce were inspired by those in the bouillabaisse in Richard Olney's book "Lulu's Provençal Table." Although white-fleshed ocean fish are traditional in such a Provençal dish (from American waters, the likes of monkfish, red snapper, rockfish, rock cod, scrod, halibut, hake, and haddock are recommended), I like to include contrasting chunks of tuna and shark—they're not only flavorful, but keep succulent when cooked. Large shrimps can be used in place of the crab meat, if you prefer. This recipe for rouille, a Provençal saffron-and-garlic mayonnaise, contains less than the usual amount of oil, yet is thick and intensely gold. The flavor of the olive oil makes or breaks the sauce. Bland, and it's a disappointment. Intense, and all you taste is oil. Lacking a balanced olive oil, I combine a fruity extra-virgin oil with a light safflower or peanut oil. With the tart, enjoy a cool, very young red wine such as a Beaujolais nouveau. Have thick slices of French bread on the table, and leafy-tipped radishes. A small

salad of peppery cresses might follow, then a block of Roquefort or fresh goat cheese. For dessert, a luscious assortment of chilled bunches of grapes. The recipe is detailed, but it's a cherishing way of enjoying fruits from the sea—in another sort of shell!

MAKES 8 SERVINGS

1½ pounds boned steaks and/or thick skinless fillets from 2 or 3 different varieties of succulent, spanking fresh ocean fish

THE FISH SEASONINGS

3 pinches of crumbled saffron threads
    or 1 pinch of ground saffron
1 garlic clove, minced
A handful of chopped wild or Florence fennel
    leaves or a good pinch of fennel seeds
Generous 1 tablespoon extra-virgin olive oil
2 tablespoons flavorful olive oil
1 large sweet onion, cut into ½-inch dice
8 medium-sized (1 pound) ripe plum tomatoes,
    cut into ½-inch dice
1 cup (about 2 ribs) sliced wild fennel;
    if unavailable, use Florence fennel or ½ cup
    each thinly sliced celery and unpeeled
    young carrots
2 cups (about 3 small) inch-sized chunks of
    unpeeled red new potatoes
1 pound raw clams or mussels in their shells
12 ounces cooked fresh crab meat or 1 pound
    raw large shrimps, peeled and deveined

THE ROUILLE

½ tablespoon crumbled saffron threads or
    ¼ teaspoon ground saffron
4½ to 6 tablespoons boiling fish stock or water
1½ cups fresh bread crumbs from an onion roll
    or French roll (remove the crusts and whirl the
    rest in a food processor or blender)
3 large garlic cloves

Hefty pinch of ground cayenne pepper, or to taste

Good pinch of sea salt, or to taste

2 small or 1½ large egg yolks

1½ cups flavorful olive oil or ¾ cup each fruity
*   extra-virgin olive oil and safflower or*
*   peanut oil*

Fully baked Short Crust Pastry shell (page 22)

1 tablespoon finely chopped shallot or onion

½ cup dry white wine

Sea salt and freshly ground white pepper, to taste

A couple of hours before planning to serve, skin the fish steaks and cut them into 1½-inch chunks; if you're using fillets, slice them into 2-inch pieces. Mix the fish seasonings on a big dish, then spread them over it. Lay the fish on top, then turn the pieces until coated. Cover and set in a cool place for about 2 hours (or in the refrigerator, if it's a hot day and/or for more than 2 hours). Turn the pieces occasionally.

In a large, heavy nonreactive skillet, heat the olive oil over medium heat. Add the onion and sauté, stirring frequently, until translucent, about 2 minutes. Add the tomatoes and fennel (or celery and carrot). Turn the heat to low and cook, uncovered, until the sauce is thick and the fennel is tender-crisp, 15 to 20 minutes. Stir occasionally. Meanwhile, steam or boil the potatoes until tender, 10 to 15 minutes. When the sauce is ready, mix in the potatoes and set aside.

Scrub the clams or mussels in 3 or 4 changes of cold water. If you're using it, tear the crab meat into large-bite-sized pieces. If you're using shrimps, cook them in boiling salted water (instead of marinade) according to the method for raw shrimps in A Shrimp Feast of a Tart on page 56. Set the shellfish aside.

To make the *rouille*, in a small bowl, steep the saffron in 4½ tablespoons stock or water for about 5 minutes. Stir in the bread crumbs and mash, adding more liquid as needed to make a loose paste. (You can make the *rouille* in a food processor or blender as you do mayonnaise, but it will lack a rustic edge.)

In a mortar with a pestle or in a bowl with a wooden spoon, combine the garlic, cayenne, and salt and mash to a paste. Add the egg yolks and pound and stir until the garlic pieces are tiny. Slowly blend in the bread paste, then stir rapidly until smooth.

Using the technique for making mayonnaise, beat the mixture constantly while adding only as much oil as it can absorb—droplets at first, then a thread, then a drizzle. You'll finish with a very thick emulsion. Taste for salt and cayenne pepper. You will have about 2 cups.

Should the *rouille* start to separate at any point, whisk in a little more of the hot fish stock or water and it will come together. Cover and refrigerate.

Ten minutes before planning to serve, set the tart shell on a heatproof platter. Place in the oven on its lowest setting to warm the shell.

Combine the shallot or onion and ¼ cup of the white wine in a nonreactive skillet large enough to accommodate the clams or mussels in a single layer. Cover and cook over high heat, shaking the skillet frequently, just until the shells open, about 5 minutes. Remove from the heat.

Meanwhile, add ¼ cup of the white wine to the tomato sauce and place the skillet over high heat. Bring to a simmer, stirring frequently. Add the fish and crab or shrimps and stir carefully until the pieces of fish are opaque—no pink in the center— and everything else is hot, about 2 minutes.

Remove from the heat. If the sauce seems dry, stir in some of the stock from the clams. Taste the sauce for seasoning.

Quickly arrange the contents of the skillet in the hot tart shell, then set the clams or mussels here and there. Mound half the *rouille* in the center, then pass the rest in a bowl. Serve the tart in wedges, heaping the filling on the pastry, then dolloping with the *rouille*.

MAKE-AHEAD NOTE: See make-ahead notes for pastries on page 19. Several hours in advance, you can cook the onion, fennel, tomatoes, and potatoes; prepare the *rouille*; and have everything else ready for cooking. The fish needs about 2 hours for seasoning. If refrigerated, bring everything to cool room temperature before proceeding.

Salt Cod Tart from the Bay of Biscay

For a zesty autumn breakfast in the sun, the day before, soak and refresh boneless, skinless salt cod (directions are on the package). Sauté finely chopped yellow onions in fruity olive oil while you roast several fat ripe tomatoes until soft. Purée the tomatoes, stir them into the onions, and then add the cod, torn into large bite-sized pieces. Cook slowly (do not boil) until succulent. Turn the mixture into a hot fully baked Short Crust Pastry shell (page 22), and arrange broad pimiento strips around the edge. Strew with a handful of coarsely chopped pieces of salt-cured olives and serve.

Tart of Chicken with Oysters in Hard-Cider Sauce

In Honor of the Months with R's

The inspiration for this tart comes from the coast of Normandy and a time when the dish could only be served six months of the year. Today, we have chicken and oysters the year around, but a hundred years ago in most of the world, there were no young chickens for the table in March and April, and no oysters from May through August. This tart offers not just a history, but also a superb blend of flavors. Make it for friends who cherish fineness. Today's palate might wish for a nontraditional finish of nutty Parmigiano Reggiano wisps on top. The exquisite sauce based on the broths of the chicken and oysters is rounded out with hard cider, the Norman wine. Before the tart, you might serve a first course of a Norman specialty in its season, either fresh asparagus or whole young green beans seasoned with butter and lemon juice. Drink sparkling cider or Muscadet. Follow the tart with a delicate salad of Bibb lettuces tossed with edible flowers, such as violets or johnny-jump-ups in early spring or calendulas in autumn. Share a perfectly ripe Pont-l'Évêque or

Camembert. For dessert, quartered apples poached and chilled in sugar syrup, served splashed with Calvados or other brandy. Buy unshucked small oysters for this very special dish. Where you can find oysters in the shell, you'll probably find someone behind the counter who'll shuck them for you.

MAKES 8 SERVINGS

2 pounds skinless, boneless chicken breasts

8 tablespoons (4 ounces) cold unsalted butter

Sea salt and freshly ground white pepper, to taste

32 fresh small oysters, shucked (about 1⅓ cups), and all their juices

Fully baked Flaky Pastry or Short Crust Pastry shell (pages 23 or 22)

2 garlic cloves, minced

Sparkling hard cider or fruity white wine to make 2 cups (about 1⅓ cups)

2 tablespoons all-purpose flour

6 large egg yolks

Heaped ⅓ cup minced parsley

A cupful of Parmigiano Reggiano cheese shavings, optional

Cut the chicken breasts lengthwise in pieces 1 inch wide and ½ inch thick. Slice the strips on the diagonal every 3 inches. Cut 4 tablespoons of the butter into 2 dozen pieces.

To serve, heat the oven to 400°F. Season the chicken with salt and white pepper while you melt 4 tablespoons of the butter in a large oven-proof skillet or shallow flameproof casserole over low heat. When it bubbles, add the chicken, turn off the heat, and stir to coat each piece with butter. Lay waxed paper on top, place in the oven, and set the timer for 6 minutes.

Meanwhile, turn the oysters and their juices into a nonreactive skillet over medium heat. Cook uncovered, stirring occasionally, until they swell and plump and their edges curl, no more than 2 minutes. Lift out with a slotted spoon into a large heated bowl. Cover with a heavy dish and set aside. Leave the broth in the skillet.

When the timer rings, check the chicken; the pieces will have plumped like the oysters. They're cooked when you press a piece with a finger and it springs back and a small cut shows the meat is white all through. Don't overcook. Lift out with a slotted spoon and add to the oysters.

Turn off the oven and set the tart shell on a heatproof serving platter in the oven to heat. Set the bowl of chicken and oysters on a thick heatproof plate and put them in the oven, covered with the dish, to keep hot.

Working quickly, pour the oyster broth through a fine strainer into a 2-cup measuring

pitcher, then add the garlic, chicken juices, and cider to make 2 cups.

Sprinkle the flour over the skillet. Slowly whisk in some of the cider mixture until you have a thin smooth paste. Whisk in the rest, then whisk over high heat until thickened. Reduce the heat and simmer 2 minutes, whisking occasionally.

In a smallish bowl, whisk the egg yolks while you blend in a little of the hot sauce. Whisk this back into the skillet. Whisk over very low heat while you add the cut-up butter a few bits at a time, waiting for those to melt before adding the next. Stir with a wooden spoon until the sauce coats it—when you run a finger down the back, the track stays. Bring just to a simmer (one bubble!), turn off the heat, and stir in the chicken, oysters, and their juices. Taste for seasoning, then very gently spoon into the tart shell. Sprinkle with the parsley, strew with the cheese shavings if you like, and serve.

MAKE-AHEAD NOTE: See make-ahead notes for pastries on page 19. The chicken and butter can be prepared for cooking a few hours in advance; the rest must be last minute. It's worth it, and goes quickly.

A Tart of Drunken Chicken

Also from France and another era: Sauté a chicken cut into parts in unsalted butter with a little chopped shallot and garlic until browned. Add generous splashes of port and dry white wine, then smaller splashes of brandy and cherry brandy. When this simmers, set aflame, shaking the skillet. Finish cooking the chicken, uncovered, then pull the meat from the bones and arrange in a hot fully baked Flaky Pastry shell (page 23). Keep the tart hot while you thicken the sauce in the skillet with heavy cream and egg yolks. Pour over the chicken, shake to settle the tart, garnish with pitted fresh cherries or red grapes and chopped chervil or parsley, and serve.

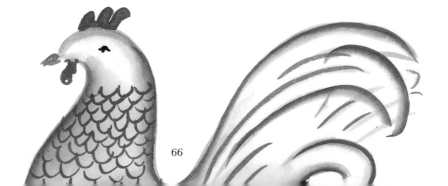

Autumn Tart of Cornish Game Hens

For Michaelmas—the Feast of the Archangel Michael

In the English countryside, pheasant is available at the local butcher. The autumn I lived in an English village, I roasted a pheasant with white grapes. It was the end of September, around the Feast of St. Michael—Michaelmas. Game meat and grapes together are the essence of autumn, and I've turned them into a tart with braised turnips—they add incomparable earthiness and sweetness. A drizzle of balsamic vinegar at the end pulls everything into focus. These days, I make the tart with Cornish game hens and serve it with a crisp watercress salad dressed with olive oil and lemon juice. I pour a berryish Zinfandel, and enjoy orange ice topped with toasted walnut halves for dessert. About technique: While roasted game hens make a beautiful presentation, the meat is most succulent steamed. It's also the easiest and fastest way of cooking poultry and the best method for preserving juices.

MAKES 8 SERVINGS

3 pounds (2 birds) Rock Cornish game hens,
    rinsed, at room temperature (reserve giblets
    for another use)

4 cups water

6 small (generous 1 pound) young turnips

Sea salt, to taste

2 tablespoons unsalted butter

½ tablespoon sugar

Heaping 1½ tablespoons all-purpose flour

Freshly ground black pepper, to taste

Fully baked Flaky Pastry shell (page 23)

2 cups (about 10 ounces) Red Flame or
    other seedless red grapes

2 to 3 tablespoons finest balsamic vinegar

6 to 8 flat-leaf parsley sprigs or celery tops

To prepare the hens, set them tails up on a fairly deep heatproof dish. Place the dish on a rack over about 3 inches of cold water in a deep pot. Bring the water to a simmer, turn the heat to medium, tightly cover the pot, and steam the birds until an instant-read thermometer inserted into the thighs registers 180°F, about 30 minutes. Once or twice while steaming, siphon up the juices in the dish into a jar. Lift out the birds to a plate. Add the rest of their juices to the jar; refrigerate it. Leave the water in the steamer.

When the birds have cooled, remove their meat in the largest possible pieces, turning the skin, bones, and trimmings into a big saucepan. Slice the breast pieces in half lengthwise. Wrap and refrigerate the meat until needed. Add the 4 cups water to the trimmings and simmer, uncovered, while you continue.

To prepare the turnips, peel them with a vegetable peeler and cut into ½-inch dice. Keep the turnips in cold water while you work so they won't discolor and work with a stainless steel knife. Pour off all but ½ inch of the hen-steaming water and lightly salt it. Add the turnips to this water, bring to a simmer, and simmer uncovered, stirring frequently, until tender, about 15 minutes. Add water if needed. If any water remains, pour it off. Add 1 tablespoon of the butter and the sugar and toss the turnips over medium-high heat until they're lightly glazed, a couple of minutes. Cover and set aside.

When the trimmings stock has developed a good flavor, strain it into the juices in the jar in the refrigerator. Melt the remaining 1 tablespoon butter in a skillet over low heat and whisk in the flour. Whisk 2 minutes. Off the heat, slowly whisk in the juices. Return to medium-high heat and whisk until thickened and smooth, about 2 minutes. Simmer over medium heat until reduced to 1¼ cups. Taste for salt and pepper.

To serve, heat the oven to 425°F. Place the shell on a pizza pan or baking sheet. Arrange the turnips over the bottom of the shell. Space the 8 breast pieces evenly over them, fanning them out from the center with their slender tips pointing toward the center. Fill in the spaces between them with the remaining meat. Spoon the sauce over the tart, then strew the grapes around the edge. Bake just until bubbly, about 25 minutes. Slide onto a heated platter. Grind over pepper, sprinkle balsamic vinegar over the meat, tuck the parsley or celery tops in the center, and serve at once.

MAKE-AHEAD NOTE: See make-ahead notes for pastries on page 19. All elements of the filling can be prepared a day in advance. Bring refrigerated ingredients to room temperature before composing the tart.

Chicken and Hearts of Artichoke Tart

Cover the bottom of a fully baked Flaky Pastry (page 23) shell with cooked rice. Fill the shell with large pieces of skinless, boneless poached chicken, cooked small artichoke hearts, and sautéed button mushrooms. Nap with a cream sauce delicately flavored with lemon zest and fresh tarragon. Shake gently to settle the sauce. Lay a sheet of brown paper on top and bake until hot. Decorate with branches of tarragon and serve.

A PUB TART

This was inspired by all the cozy slices I ate in pubs in London's Covent Garden. To drink with the tart, you'll need ale, bitters, or ginger beer. Serve a crisp salad—perhaps coleslaw—offer Stilton cheese afterward, and finish with vanilla ice cream topped with hot rum and raisins. The best sausages will have no fillers (bread and such) or preservatives.

MAKES 8 SERVINGS

10 ounces uncooked veal or lean pork sausages,
    sliced crosswise ¼ inch thick

4 ounces boneless, fat-free pork, cut into
    ½-inch dice

2 medium-large (1 ¾ pounds) red onions,
    chopped

¼ pound boneless, fat-free ham steak, cut into
    ½-inch dice

1 medium-large green apple, unpeeled, cored,
    and cut into ½-inch dice

Rounded 3 tablespoons chopped fresh or
    1 tablespoon crumbled dried sage leaves

Sea salt and freshly ground black pepper, to taste

2 smallish eggs, beaten until blended

1 tablespoon butter, softened

Unbaked Short Crust Pastry shell (page 22)

A handful of finely chopped parsley

A decorative pig or apple cut from the dough
    trimmings and baked (400°F) until lightly
    browned, optional

In a large, heavy dry skillet over medium heat, sauté the sausages and pork, stirring frequently, until cooked, 15 to 17 minutes. Using a slotted spoon, remove to a mixing bowl. Add the onions to the drippings in the skillet and sauté over high heat, stirring almost constantly, until softened, 2 to 3 minutes.

To serve, heat the oven to 400°F. Add the ham, apple, and sage to the onions in the skillet and sauté until fragrant, about 5 minutes. Blend the onion mixture with the sausage and pork, then taste for salt and pepper. Add the eggs and blend in thoroughly.

Brush the tart shell in its mold with the butter, then arrange the filling in it, making a smooth place in the center that will be for the pastry pig or apple. Bake until browned and bubbly, about 45 minutes. Unmold, then slide onto a heated platter, then lift off the ring. Sprinkle with the parsley, set the decoration on top, and serve.

MAKE-AHEAD NOTE: See make-ahead notes for pastries on page 19. The pastry can be ready in the pan, the pastry decoration baked, and the sausage, pork, and onions cooked several hours in advance. If you refrigerate the latter, bring them to room temperature before finishing.

A Cornish Flan

Inspired by Cornish pasties: Fill a partially baked Short Crust Pastry shell (page 22) with a layer of thinly sliced cooked potatoes, then a layer of thinly sliced cooked turnips, then a layer of crumbled raw ground ultra-lean beef, seasoning well all the way up. Strew with chopped raw onions, dot with butter, and bake until the meat is cooked. Serve hot or take, cooled, on a picnic.

Scottish Steak, Mushroom, and Pearl Onion Tart

For Hogmanay—Scottish New Year's Eve

Easily made, this classic stew in a tart shell is perfect for celebrating Scottish New Year's Eve. Pour that long-awaited Saint-Emilion or Cabernet Sauvignon. After the tart, have a crunchy romaine salad and aged Cheddar cheese, and for dessert, a bonny custard piped with whipped cream and decorated with candied angelica and glacé cherries.

MAKES 8 SERVINGS

2 pounds tender, flavorful, fat-free stewing beef (chuck or round), cut into 1-inch cubes

¼ cup all-purpose flour

Scant 2 teaspoons sea salt, or to taste

Freshly ground black pepper, to taste

2 tablespoons lard (or use mild-tasting oil)

1 pound fresh mushrooms, each 2 inches in diameter, cut into quarters

About 3¼ cups (1 pound) blanched and peeled pearl onions (see directions on page 52)

1 pint premium malt liquor

2 tablespoons Madeira or port

1½ cups chopped parsley, preferably flat-leaf

Unbaked Short Crust Pastry shell (page 22)

Decorative autumn leaves cut from the dough trimmings and baked (400°F) until lightly browned, optional

In a paper bag, shake the beef with the flour, salt, and pepper until the cubes are fairly evenly coated.

Heat 1 tablespoon of the lard in a large heavy skillet (cast iron is ideal) over medium-high heat. Add the beef and sauté, stirring frequently, until all sides have darkened and a bit of creamy gravy has formed in the pan, about 10 minutes. Scrape the contents of the skillet into a bowl.

Without washing it, return the pan to the heat. Melt the remaining spoonful of lard and add the mushrooms. Stir them almost constantly until glossy and brown, 6 to 7 minutes. Add to the meat. Again without washing it, add the onions to the dry skillet and sauté them, stirring, until browned, about 2 minutes.

Remove from the heat and stir in the malt liquor, scraping up caramelized bits. Return the meat and mushrooms and every scrap of gravy to the skillet. Cover, turn heat to lowest, and simmer, stirring frequently, until the meat is on the brink of tenderness and the sauce has reduced considerably, about 1½ hours. Blend in the Madeira, then taste for salt and pepper. Set the lid askew, and cool in a cold place.

To bake, heat the oven to 400°F. Mix half the parsley into the stew and smooth it into the shell in its mold. Lay a 12-inch square of buttered brown paper, buttered side down, on top. This keeps the meat moist but permits the pastry to bake without steaming. Bake until the crust is lightly browned and the stew bubbling, about 40 minutes.

Unmold and slide onto a hot platter. Sprinkle with the remaining parsley, arrange the pastry leaves on top, and serve.

MAKE-AHEAD NOTE: See make-ahead notes for pastries on page 19. The leaves can be baked and the filling can be prepared a day in advance, but bring the filling to room temperature before baking.

Tartlets of Pâté de Foie Gras

Cut blocks of prepared *pâté de foie gras* or any fine pâté and tuck into very small, fully baked Flaky Pastry (page 23) tartlet shells, leaving a ⅛ inch margin below the rim. Lay a flat sprig of chervil or parsley on top, and spoon beef consommé the gloppy consistency of egg white over the top. Chill until set and serve within a few hours.

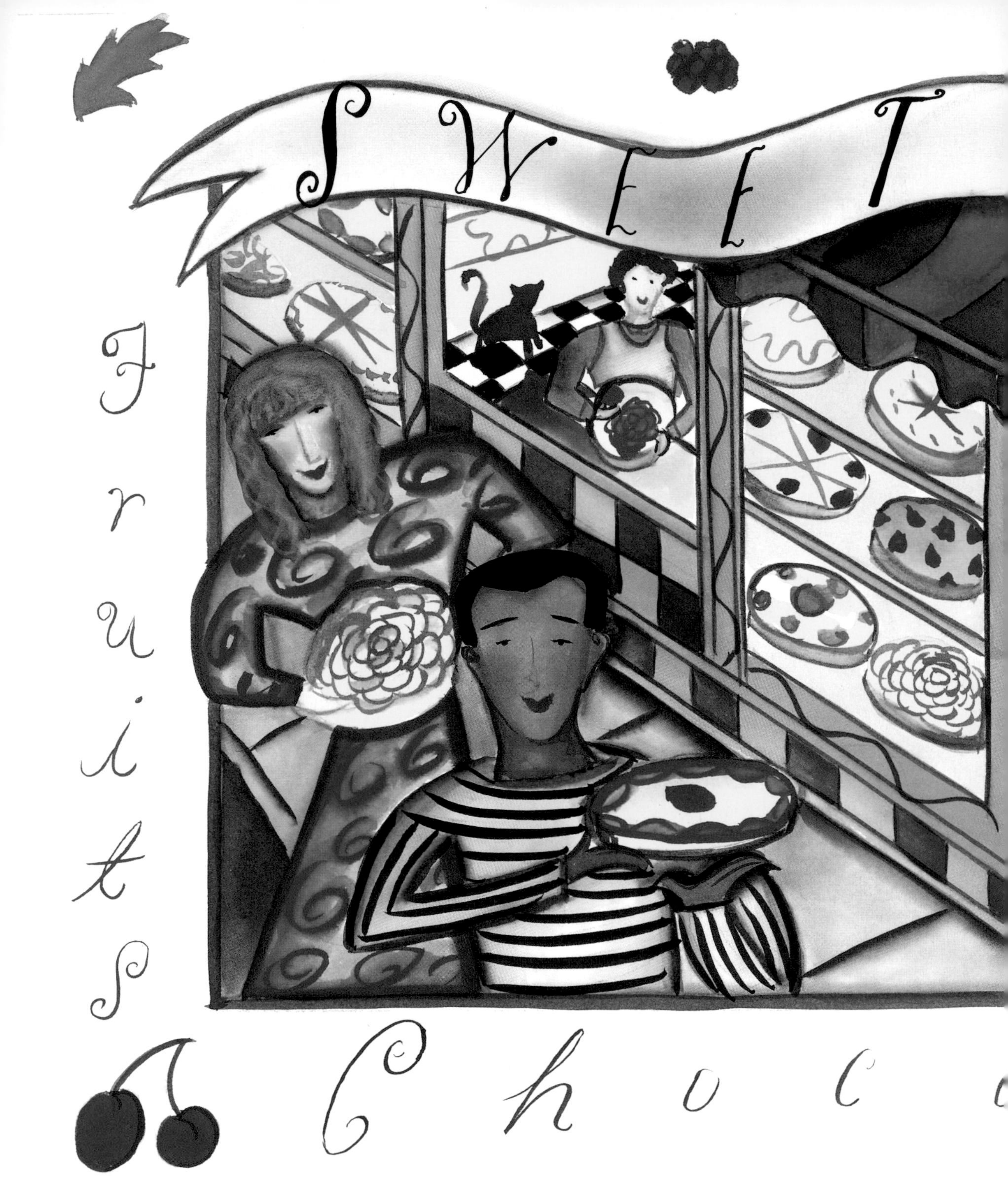
SWEET
Fruits
Choc

90
FIGGY MACAROON TARTLETS
IN COMMEMORATION OF THE EXPULSION FROM THE GARDEN OF EDEN
Here are sweet pastry tartlets of featherlight macaroon cake, strawberry jam, and a voluptuous glazed purple fig.

92
BEAUJOLAIS PEAR TART
IN PRAISE OF LOUIS XIV'S LONGEVITY—HE LOVED HIS PEARS AND HE REIGNED 77 YEARS
In a flaky pastry shell lined with raspberry preserves, translucent wine-red pears are set off by ivory custard, green pistachios, and a furled lemon zest rose.

95
BLACK WALNUT MERINGUE TART
FOR HALLOWE'EN
A crispy meringue shell is filled with sherried whipped cream, black walnuts, and orange chrysanthemums.

97
TAFFETY TART
IN HONOR OF WILLIAM TELL
What appears to be a simple apple tart is actually chunky applesauce topped with honeyed and orange-brandied pieces of mandarins and lemons beneath overlapping slices of apples glazed with pale jelly.

100
TARTLETS OF BRANDIED GINGERY MINCE
FOR TWELFTH NIGHT
Crystallized ginger, walnuts, candied orange peel, and a nip of brandy are blended into mincemeat, then tucked into tartlets of sweet pastry. Evergreen sprigs decorate the tray.

Rhubarb Tart with Rhubarb Fool

For April Fool's Day

The sensational colors—pale and bright pinks—the balance of sweet and tart, the melting soft fruit against the cloud of cream against the crunchy crust make this tart proof that we're nobody's fools! The spicy sweetness of a chilled Moscato di Canelli would be lovely to sip with this luscious dessert. The amount of poached rhubarb in the bottom of the tart is a matter of taste. I'm happy with the following proportions—about 4 cups cooked rhubarb to 3 cups fool—but a friend wished for much more. There's room for about half again as much poached fruit, so if you like, prepare 4½ pounds of rhubarb. The 1 cup for the fool should stay the same. Increase the poaching water, sugar, orange zest, and lemon juice by half. Save the brilliant poaching syrup to make rhubarb coolers: Splash the syrup over ice in a tall glass and add club soda to the top, an idea of Deborah Madison's.

MAKES 8 TO 10 SERVINGS

3 cups water

1½ cups sugar

Shredded zest of 1 large orange

3 tablespoons fresh lemon juice

Nine 12- to 14-inch long, inch-wide (2½ pounds)
  crisp red rhubarb stalks, cut into ½-inch
  pieces (about 5 cups)

Fully baked Crunchy Graham-Pecan Crumb
  Crust (page 25) in its mold

1 cup cold heavy cream, whipped until stiff

An unsprayed springtime fruit blossom with its
  leaves, for garnish

In a large nonreactive skillet, bring the water and
sugar to a boil, stirring until the sugar dissolves.
Stir in the orange zest, lemon juice, and then the
rhubarb. Poach, uncovered, over medium-high
heat until the fruit is thoroughly tender, 7 to 8
minutes. Stir occasionally. Set the lid on askew
and set in the refrigerator until very cold.

Up to 3 or 4 hours before serving, pour the
rhubarb into a large sieve over a bowl. Shake the
sieve until the rhubarb is firm. Set aside 1 cup
rhubarb for the fool and spread the rest over the
bottom of the shell.

To make the fool, fold the reserved rhubarb
into the whipped cream. It needn't be thoroughly
blended—in fact streaks of the fruit through the
cream are delicious. Leaving an inch of the pink
rhubarb showing around the edge of the tart, swirl
the fool over the top. Lift off the ring and slide the
tart onto a platter. Set the blossom in the center
and serve.

MAKE-AHEAD NOTE: The shell can be baked a
day in advance. The rhubarb should be poached
at least 8 hours in advance, then it can be strained
a few hours before serving and returned to the
refrigerator. The cream can be whipped hours in
advance, but whisk it until fluffy before making
the fool. Once the fool has been made, serve
immediately.

A Lover's Tart

Arrange luscious kiwifruit slices in a swirling pattern to fill in a Meringue Shell (page 27). Sprinkle
with framboise, border with small strawberries,
and glaze the tart with melted strawberry jelly.

Rosy Strawberry Tart

Simple perfection. When you gather the flowers, don't handle the petals you'll be candying (they crease easily), and keep them dry. If unsprayed roses aren't available when you need them, knock on the door of the most passionate gardener in your neighborhood and ask to borrow a couple of cups of English daisies or violas. A young, light, sweet Moselle is wonderful with strawberries. If you don't have time to candy the petals, the tart will still be a feast for the eyes.

MAKES 8 SERVINGS

½ recipe custard in Beaujolais Pear Tart
    (page 92)
1 egg white
½ teaspoon water
½ teaspoon rose water
Superfine sugar (purchased or pulverize
    granulated sugar in a blender)
30 to 35 small unsprayed, sweetly scented fresh
    pink or red rose petals

Fully baked Crisp Sweet Pastry shell (page 24)
1 tablespoon unsalted butter, softened
48 large, 64 medium-sized, 80 small,
    or a mixture of sizes (about 4 pint baskets) of
    fine sweet ripe strawberries, hulled
Generous ¾ cup strawberry jelly

Prepare the custard as directed, then cool.

To candy the rose petals (you can do this with whole flowers, too), in a bowl, use a fork to stir the egg white with the water and rose water until the white is loosened and lightly frothy. Pour about ½ cup superfine sugar onto a large plate. Get out your cake rack. Holding each rose petal at its base over the bowl, use a delicate brush to paint a light veil of egg white on both sides of the petal. Now hold the petal over the plate and use a teaspoon to sprinkle the petal with sugar all over—you want to be able to see the petal through the veil. Set on the rack until thoroughly dry, then store in a tightly capped glass jar.

To serve, set the pastry shell on a platter. Gently moistureproof the bottom of the shell by brushing it with the butter. Smooth in the custard. Fill the tart with circles of whole strawberries, hulled ends down, fitting them as closely as you can get them: Make the first circle against the outside edge, then make smaller and smaller circles until you set 1 perfect berry in the center. If your berries are different sizes, mix them up in the circles all over the tart. It's not handsomer to have one row of tall berries descending toward small ones. Don't worry if you need to move a berry now and then—just smooth the custard beneath with a fingertip.

When the tart's full, in the microwave or in a small pan over low heat, melt the jelly and spoon it over the berries as a glaze. Don't miss a spot. Immediately set the petals in groups of 5 around the tart, starting in the center and tucking their bases down among the berries. Let the clusters of petals resemble wild single-petal roses. Let the size of the petals determine the number of clusters you make.

MAKE-AHEAD NOTE: See make-ahead notes for pastries on page 19. So it will be thick and cold, prepare the custard at least 8 hours and up to 24 hours before serving. Depending on how damp the air is, the rose petals are their best within 3 to 6 hours of candying. If it must, the tart can wait a couple of hours before serving. But if everything's ready, it goes together quickly.

Rummy Caramelized Pineapple Ice Cream Tart

Just before serving, spread softened fine vanilla ice cream or frozen yogurt over the bottom of a fully baked Spiced Crisp Sweet Pastry shell flavored with ginger (page 25). Dredge bite-sized chunks of fresh pineapple in sugar, then toss in a nonstick skillet over high heat with broken pieces of toasted pecans until the sugar caramelizes. Spoon the hot mixture over the ice cream, then drizzle with dark rum, dust with cinnamon, decorate with a bright unsprayed flower, and serve.

March Pane Tarte of Aprecox

When I read about Elizabeth I's passion for march pane—marzipan—and apricots, I wanted to taste them together, so I composed this tart. The buttery custardlike filling billows up and envelopes the apricots—soft against melting crisp pastry. This may be the most toothsome apricot tart you've ever tasted. After dinner, thimblefuls of an apricot liqueur will let the pleasure linger.

MAKES 10 SERVINGS

THE MARCH PANE

8 tablespoons (4 ounces) unsalted butter,
   softened and cut into small pieces

1¾ cups confectioners' sugar

1 extra-large egg

1 tablespoon egg white

3 to 4 tablespoons brandy, plus more for the glaze

¼ teaspoon pure almond extract

1 cup plus 2 tablespoons (4 ounces) lightly
   packed ground toasted almonds

2 tablespoons cornstarch

Partially baked Crisp Sweet Pastry shell
   (page 24)

3 tablespoons fine dried bread crumbs
   or unsalted cracker crumbs

10 to 12 medium-sized fragrant, firm apricots,
   cut in half along their seam line and pitted

⅓ cup puréed apricot preserves

8 unsprayed bright orange, purple, crimson,
   yellow, white, blue, and/or black pansies
   with sprigs of their leaves

In a food processor or with a mixer, cream together the butter and confectioners' sugar until fluffy. One at a time, add the whole egg, egg white, brandy, and almond extract, blending thoroughly after each addition. Blend the almonds and cornstarch together and add them, then process or beat just until smooth. Wrap this march pane tightly and chill.

To make the tart, heat the oven to 400°F. Place the tart shell in its mold on a pizza pan or baking sheet. Sprinkle the bottom of the shell with the crumbs. With a fingertip, smooth the march pane evenly over the bottom. Starting around the outside, snugly fit apricot halves on top, cut sides down, finishing with one perfect half in the center. Bake 10 minutes, then turn the heat to 350°F. Continue to bake until the march pane is the color of macaroons, about 30 minutes more.

Meanwhile, in a small vessel over low heat or in the microwave, warm the preserves and enough brandy to make a thick glaze. Cover to keep warm and loose.

Slide the baked tart in its mold onto a cooling rack. Spoon over a veil of glaze (the surface probably will be uneven—don't worry if it is). Cool about 10 minutes more, then unmold. As soon as the tart is at room temperature, slide it onto a doily-lined platter. Decorate with pansies and their leaves and serve.

MAKE-AHEAD NOTE: See make-ahead notes for pastries on page 19. The march pane may be prepared a day or two in advance and refrigerated. Serve the tart no later than 6 hours after baking.

Turkish Apricot Tart

In winter, gently poach halves of best-quality large dried apricots in sugar syrup (as for the rhubarb in the Rhubarb Tart with Rhubarb Fool, page 79) with the zest of a lemon until tender and plump. Lift out the apricots, blot dry, and let cool. Just before serving, spread the bottom of a fully baked Crisp Sweet Pastry shell (page 24) with warmed apricot preserves. Fill the tart with whipped cream folded into thick plain yogurt sweetened with melted honey. Set the apricots on top, cut sides down, strew with chopped toasted pistachios—and pomegranate seeds, if in season—and sprinkle with rose water from a salt shaker. Serve at once.

Essence of a Summer Fruit Tart

For me, it isn't summer until I've eaten more than my share of a glorious fresh fruit tart. The Fourth of July is the perfect time for this, because apricots and cherries are still going strong, every imaginable berry is ripening, and nectarines, peaches, and plums are in the ascendance. What's wonderful is that the flavor of these fruits is even more intense when lightly cooked than raw—same thing happens to their colors. I make this tart simply. Prepared with just apricots, there's a rich apricot flavor. With the crimson juices and orbs of sweet cherries added, the mingled flavors and colors are divine. Include berries and plums, and it's heaven. Then when every drop and crumb is gone, go outdoors and sip blackberry brandy in the moonlight. It's hard to tell you the amount you'll need to fill the tart, since fruits fit together differently. A dozen apricots and two dozen pitted sweet cherries are about right. If you want to get it exactly right, cut out a piece of paper the size of the shell, then you can arrange fruits on it at the market and buy just the right

amount. If the fruits are really juicy, and if it's available, line the bottom with thin sheets of sponge cake (page 16).

MAKES 10 SERVINGS

Partially baked Spiced Crisp Sweet Pastry shell made with cinnamon and/or mace (page 25)
½ cup apricot preserves
About 6 cups prepared—(1½ pounds)—small, ripe, perfumed and handsome fruits, all of one sort, of two different sorts, or of several: apricots, sweet cherries, dark and light plums, nectarines, peaches, and every berry but strawberries (not at their best cooked)
Rounded ¼ cup vanilla sugar or ¼ cup granulated sugar blended with ⅛ teaspoon pure vanilla extract
1 quart vanilla ice cream or frozen yogurt

Position a rack in the top of the oven and heat to 400°F. Smooth the preserves over the bottom of the tart shell. Cut the small stone fruits in half through the center. Remove the pit but don't peel. Pit the cherries and leave whole. Cut the large fruit in big chunks.

Fill the shell with the larger fruits, *cut sides up*, then fill the spaces with the smaller fruits. Sprinkle the sugar over the top. Set the shell on a pizza pan or baking sheet and place on the top rack of the oven. Bake until some of the sugar has caramelized, about 25 minutes.

Let cool about 15 minutes, then serve warm dolloped with something icy and vanilla. The fruits are their own decoration.

MAKE-AHEAD NOTE: See make-ahead notes for pastries on page 19. So it won't be the least bit soggy, bake the tart no more than a couple of hours before serving.

Tropical Fruit Tart

On the bottom of a fully baked Crisp Sweet Pastry shell (page 24), make a thin bed of lightly sweetened cream cheese flavored with well-drained, finely chopped fresh pineapple. On top, arrange a pinwheel of overlapping mango slices fanning them out from the center to the edge of the tart. Heap raspberries in the center, overlap peeled kiwifruit slices around the berries, then, at the edge, make a border of fresh mint leaves. Serve within the hour.

CROSTATA DI MARMELLATA

The Italian word "crostata" translates as "pie," but in Rome, "crostata" means a flat, lattice-topped pastry filled with preserves. The classic is "crostata di visciole," with preserves made of the small, dark sour cherries grown in what's left of the Roman countryside. When the preserves you've made or treated yourself to are fabulous, make a classic crostata: Use the Crisp Sweet Pastry on page 24, doubling the amount of ingredients. Roll out the dough into a 10-inch round ⅛ inch thick. Spread with jam as directed in the following recipe. Roll out the remaining dough the same thickness and cut 12 lattice strips ½ inch wide. Lay a strip ½ inch in from either edge of the round. Set 4 more strips 1½ inches apart from them and one another. Turn the tart just enough so that when you lay 6 strips as before, they form elegant diamonds—place the first strip on top of one of the center strips. Roll the remaining dough into a 32-inch strip and lay it flat around the edge (patching as needed), to make a finished border. Brush the strips with beaten egg yolk,

and bake as for the hazelnut pastry *crostata*. While a *crostata* is always simple, every baker has his or her version. You'll create your own style with your choice of pastry and how you make the lattice strips. My style is rustic—the pastry is warmly colored and flavored with ground hazelnuts, the strips are an insouciant inch wide, the lattice is in no-nonsense squares, and a chunk of fresh fruit glints from each square. It's not traditional to set fruit on the jam, but I do. Any fresh fruit that bakes well and any fine-quality jam or preserves—whether of the same fruit or one that's complementary—are right for a *crostata*. In winter, I lay cuts of pineapple over apricot jam. Play with *crostata* possibilities! After your first *crostata*, you'll be making them hand over fist. Even beginners can make this tart. Although the hazelnut dough takes coaxing, it's more forgiving than most other doughs. You don't even need a tart pan. Heavy foil and a baking sheet are all that's wanted. Finally, when this jolly tart is for a super-festive occasion, I decorate it with leaves of chocolate and pass a bottle of Frangelico liqueur.

MAKES 10 TO 12 SERVINGS

European Hazelnut Pastry dough (page 26)
About 1⅔ cups seedless blackberry jam
21 (a scant 1¼ cups, about 10 ounces) very
*   large blackberries or similar pieces of fruit*
1 large egg yolk
A pinch of salt
A little granulated sugar

THE CHOCOLATE LEAVES, OPTIONAL
About 1½ ounces bittersweet or semisweet
*   chocolate, melted and cooled (page 9)*
24 smallish unsprayed rose or citrus leaves

A little sifted confectioners' sugar

Set an 18-inch square of heavy aluminum foil (shiny side up) on a baking sheet that has one rimless side, or set it on a rimmed baking sheet turned upside down.

Roll out half the dough between sheets of waxed paper into a ³⁄₁₆-inch-thick round. Using a template (a skillet or such), trim the round to 11 inches in diameter. Pull off one sheet of the paper and use the other to lift the dough onto the foil. Roll again if necessary to make the round symmetrical.

Smooth the jam ½ inch thick over the round, stopping 1 inch shy of the edge. Knead dough scraps into the remaining dough and roll out ³⁄₁₆ inch thick into a rectangle 12 inches long. Cut lengthwise into 8 strips, each 1 inch wide.

To easily space 4 broad lattice strips, mark the center of the tart on the foil. Then, ¾ inch to

88

one side of this mark, draw an X 1 inch wide. Draw 3 more such X's 1½ inches apart, one to one side, and two to the other side. Using the support of a table knife, lift up the strips, one at a time, and, starting at the edge of the round (the strips will go over the bare inch of border), lay a strip straight down the tart at each X. When the strips break (and they will), just press and smooth the ends together (no water for glue). Give the tart a quarter turn and repeat with 4 more strips to make squares.

Press together the dough scraps and roll out as before into a rectangle 12 inches long and ³⁄₁₆-inch thick. This time cut 3 strips lengthwise, each ¾ inch wide. Fit the strips around the edge to make a finishing band. With a fork or the tip of a spoon, press this band, any strip between, and the base together to seal securely and make a decorative trim.

Beat the yolk and salt in a small dish, then brush it over all the dough. Try not to drip any into the jam. Refrigerate for 1 hour.

To bake, heat the oven to 375°F. Set a berry (or piece of fresh fruit) in the center of each lattice square. Tuck the smallest fruits in the fractions of squares at the edges. Sprinkle each with a few grains of granulated sugar. Bake until golden brown, about 25 minutes (this pastry bakes quickly). Remove from the oven and don't disturb the tart for 15 minutes, then carefully slide the foil off the pan onto a rack to cool completely.

For the chocolate leaves, brush the undersides of the rose or citrus leaves (the veining is more prominent there) with a layer of chocolate a scant ¹⁄₁₆ inch thick—thick enough to make the leaves handleable, but thin enough to make them realistic. Lay them over a rolling pin (so they'll curve realistically) and chill until set. Carefully peel each green leaf away, leaving a chocolate leaf. You can store the leaves between layers of waxed paper in a tightly covered box in a cool place.

To serve, slide the tart onto a platter or tray. Dust the top *very lightly* with confectioners' sugar shaken through a sieve. Set a pair of chocolate leaves around the edge of the tart to mark each serving—10 or 12, depending on the menu and the guests.

MAKE-AHEAD NOTE: See make-ahead notes for pastries on page 19. This tart is equally good—may be even better—the day after baking. The chocolate leaves can be prepared a week or two in advance.

Jam Tartlets Inspired by Joan Miró

Line tartlet molds with thinly rolled European Hazelnut Pastry (page 26) and bake blind, fully. Reroll the trimmings and cut out and bake hearts, stars, cows, cats, or roses—any shape appropriate to the occasion. Fill each tart with a different color of jam or preserves, then return to the oven just until the jam has melted in place. Cool and serve with a cutout set on each tart.

Figgy Macaroon Tartlets

In Commemoration of the Expulsion from the Garden of Eden

These delightful tartlets are superb pastry with a light, almost cakey center. Perfect for a reflective evening with friends and a tipple of amaretto. Out of season, summer's fig can be replaced with any handsome fresh, glacé, or poached fruit. Glaze with a jelly of the appropriate color.

MAKES SIXTEEN 2-1/2-INCH TARTLETS

1 ¾ cups (5 ounces) sliced almonds, toasted
8 tablespoons (4 ounces) unsalted butter, softened
½ cup plus 2 teaspoons sugar
1 tablespoon pure vanilla extract
2 large egg whites
Pinch of salt
16 fully baked Crisp Sweet Pastry (page 24)
   2½-inch tartlet shells

¾ cup strawberry jam or other desired jam
8 ripe purple figs, sliced in half lengthwise,
   or 16 small slices of other fresh, glacé,
   or poached fruits
1 cup red currant jelly or pale jelly, melted
Unsprayed fresh fig leaves or other
   decorative leaves

In a food processor, grind the almonds. You'll have 1¼ cups. Add the butter and process until fully blended. With the motor running, slowly add the ½ cup sugar. When blended and fluffy, add the vanilla and process until smooth.

Heat the oven to 375°F. In a bowl, beat the egg whites with the salt until foamy. Slowly add the 2 teaspoons sugar and beat just until the mixture holds its shape softly when you lift the beaters. Thoroughly mix about one-third of the egg whites into the butter mixture to lighten it. Add the rest of the egg whites and fold them in just until there are no more puffs of white.

Set the tartlet shells on a baking sheet. Divide the almond mixture among them—about 2 tablespoons each—smoothing the tops. Bake until a toothpick inserted into the center emerges clean, about 15 minutes. Gently slip the tartlets onto a rack and let cool thoroughly.

Spread the top of each tartlet with jam, then center half a fig (or a piece of fruit) on it, cut side down. Spoon the jelly over the fruit to glaze it. Serve the tartlets within a few hours, using leaves as doilies.

MAKE-AHEAD NOTE: See make ahead notes for pastries on page 19. The tartlets, without any jam on them, keep beautifully for several days.

Tart of Wild Plums

All over this country—not that far from where you live—there are wild plums you can harvest for a tart. Go on a plum-hunting picnic, then bring back a basketful of small red or yellow or purple fruits and stew them up with sugar and orange and lemon zest. If you end up with more pits than flesh, well, this is not just about eating—it's a tart adventure! You and a friend can pick out the pits. Then, in the bottom of a fully baked Short Crust or Crisp Sweet Pastry shell (page 22 and page 24, respectively), sprinkle a generous amount of chopped toasted hazelnuts, butternuts, macadamia nuts, or walnuts. Smooth in your cooked plums in whatever shape they're in, give a shake of cinnamon, a drizzle of butter—more sugar?—and then sit down and spoon it up, a reflection of all good things.

BEAUJOLAIS PEAR TART

IN PRAISE OF LOUIS XIV'S LONGEVITY—HE LOVED HIS PEARS AND HE REIGNED 77 YEARS

This is a pure tart made of six elements that combine to give exquisite flavor, color, texture, and shape. Sips of clear, pungent pear eau-de-vie when the tart has been eaten are in keeping. Pear poaching is usually done on top of the stove, but the oven's embracing heat poaches large pieces of fruit more gently, and requires no attention.

MAKES 8 SERVINGS

THE PEARS

5 Bosc or Anjou pears, all the same size and
　　shape (you'll need 4, but it's wise to have one
　　for backup)
Zest of 1 lemon, removed with a vegetable peeler
1 fifth less ½ cup (tipple for the cook)
　　Beaujolais or Gamay Beaujolais
1¼ cups water
Heaping ¾ cup sugar

THE CUSTARD

1½ cups heavy cream
1½ cups half-and-half
5 tablespoons sugar
7 large egg yolks
2 teaspoons pure vanilla extract

Zest of 1 large lemon, removed with a
　　vegetable peeler in one piece about
　　½ inch wide, if possible
Fully baked Flaky Pastry shell (page 23)
¼ cup raspberry preserves
Rounded ⅓ cup roasted pistachio halves

To prepare the pears, peel them with a vegetable peeler. Slice them in half, top to bottom, cutting through their thinnest side so the halves lie as flat as possible. Use an apple corer or small paring knife to remove the core.

If you have time, score the pears to form a handsome decoration that emphasizes the pear's sensuous shape: With the tip of a small knife, run a line about ¼ inch deep down the center of the pear on the rounded side. Run 2 lines similarly on either side of this line, following the outside curve.

Heat the oven to 375°F.

Line up the halves, cut sides down, on your counter. Using the vegetable peeler, pare down any tops that stick up, so all are the same height.

Arrange the pears, cut sides up, in a shallow 9-inch baking dish. Add the lemon zest. In a non-reactive skillet over medium-high heat, heat the wine, water, and sugar, stirring until the sugar dissolves. When it starts to simmer, pour it over the pears. Place the dish in the oven, set a lid on askew, and bake until the pears test tender with a thin skewer or toothpick and they're beginning to become translucent, 1¼ to 1½ hours. Remove to a cool place. Leave the pears in the syrup until you need them.

To make the custard, combine the cream, half-and-half, and sugar in a heavy-bottomed saucepan and heat over medium heat, stirring occasionally, until a skin forms. Discard the skin. Meanwhile, in a bowl, stir the egg yolks with a fork until blended. Very slowly whisk in about 1 cup of the hot cream; when smooth, whisk this mixture back into the cream in the saucepan. Turn the heat to low and stir constantly and all across the bottom with a wooden spatula or spoon. Look at the back of your spoon now—the mixture is a thin *veil*. When the custard makes an opaque *coating* on the back of the spoon—run your finger through it and the track stays—it's cooked, 5 to 7 minutes. Should you suddenly see specks of white in the custard, you've over-cooked it: Pour it at once into a blender and whirl it until smooth.

Remove the custard from the heat at once and pour it through a fine-mesh sieve into a bowl large enough so the sauce is only a couple of inches deep. Stir in the vanilla. Lay plastic wrap directly on the surface and refrigerate until very cold, 12 to 24 hours. Stir briefly before serving.

To make the rose for decorating the tart, follow the natural curl of the lemon zest strip: Make a little cone, point down, at the beginning of the strip, pinching the bottom. Now just wind the rest of the strip around and around, rather tightly at first, then more loosely, catching the layers and pinching them to hold them in place. If the piece breaks, just add it where it was, pinching to hold it, and keep winding. At the end, you'll have a rose. Set it down and pick it up carefully, to preserve the lovely shape.

To serve, using a slotted spoon, transfer the pears, cut sides down, to a towel to drain dry. Set the tart shell on its serving platter. Use a tablespoon to smooth the preserves evenly over the bottom of the shell. Pour about 1⅓ cups of the

custard sauce into the bottom, directing it first into a tablespoon, which will break its fall, so the preserves won't be dislodged. Arrange the pear halves evenly in the sauce, fanning them out around the shell, slender ends pointing toward the center. (If you spatter any sauce on the pears, wipe it off.) Strew the tart with pistachios, set the rose in the center, and serve at once, passing the rest of the sauce in a pitcher.

MAKE-AHEAD NOTE: See make-ahead notes for pastries on page 19. Every element except the rose can be prepared the day before composing the tart. So it won't be soggy, the tart must be put together just before serving.

Tart of Seckel Pears and Walnuts with Caramel

In a baking dish, copiously strew peeled, cored ripe Seckel pear halves, cut sides up, with butter and sugar. Cover and bake until tender. Spread the bottom of a fully baked Flaky Pastry shell (page 23) with raspberry preserves. Arrange the pears on it, cut sides down, fanning them out from the center. Make a sugar syrup (page 9) using double the amount of sugar. Pour off the baking juices into the syrup and add a big handful of toasted walnut halves. Simmer until the syrup is a rich caramel color. Pour over the pears and serve at once, passing crème fraîche or sour cream on the side.

Black Walnut Meringue Tart

My friend Cathy Turney is famous for this dessert. As she notes on the recipe card, "This sounds rich but for some reason it doesn't seem so." Enjoy glasses of the same sherry that's in the whipped cream. If you're not used to the musky taste of black walnuts, you may want to use English walnuts instead. You can double the amount, since they contain half as much flavor.

MAKES 8 SERVINGS

Meringue Shell (page 27)
1 cup (4½ ounces) black walnuts,
   toasted and chopped
1⅓ cups cold heavy cream
⅓ to ⅔ cup sweet sherry such as an amoroso,
   according to taste
A handful of unsprayed orange button or other
   chrysanthemums, for garnish

Prepare the meringue shell to the point where you've combined the remaining sugar and saltines and beaten them into the meringue. Sprinkle ⅔ cup of the walnuts over the mixture and fold them in with a large rubber spatula until thoroughly blended. Smooth the mixture into the mold and finish the recipe as directed.

To serve, in a bowl, whip the cream until stiff and blend in the sherry. Pile the cream in the shell, mounding it slightly in the center. Sprinkle over the remaining walnuts and strew with the flowers. Serve at once in wedges.

MAKE-AHEAD NOTE: See the keeping notes for the shell on page 19. The cream can be beaten an hour or two before serving. Whisk it again to revive it before piling it into the shell.

Frozen Zabaglione Fruit Tart

This is delectable, easy, and fast any time of the year. From 3 to 36 hours in advance, prepare your favorite zabaglione (aka sabayon) recipe. When the custard is thick and forms wonderfully airy mounds, set the pot in a bowl of ice and beat until cold. In a bowl, beat cold heavy cream—about half the volume of the zabaglione—until stiff and fold into the zabaglione. Freeze without stirring in a covered metal pan. An hour before serving, spread the bottom of a fully baked Crisp Sweet Pastry shell (page 24) with not-too-sweet preserves, such as apricot, cherry, raspberry, strawberry, or plum. To serve, fill the shell with sweetened slices or berries of a complementary fruit. Quickly scoop up the frozen zabaglione with a large spoon and set scoops over the fruit. Sprinkle with grated orange or lemon zest or sweet chocolate shavings and serve at once.

TAFFETY TART

IN HONOR OF WILLIAM TELL

Aka Orangeado, Andalusian, and Florentine tart, this tart from the eighteenth century honors William Tell because, at first glance, it's a classic European apple tart with circles of overlapping apple slices beneath a shimmering glaze. But cut a slice and you'll find that beneath the apples is a layer of tender tangerine and lemon slices. Chunky applesauce beneath the citrus adds a delicious balance to the other flavors and textures. After coffee, serve one of the delectable mandarin liqueurs to echo the dessert. Preparing the tangerines and lemons takes a little time. If you're rushed, blend 1 cup chunky lemon marmalade and 1 cup chunky orange marmalade and omit the honey and orange liqueur.

MAKES 8 TO 10 SERVINGS

Crisp Sweet Pastry dough (page 24)

2 (8 ounces) tangerines or sweet oranges, unpeeled

2 (8 ounces) Meyer or other sweet lemons, unpeeled

¼ cup light honey

¼ cup orange-flavored liqueur

1½ tablespoons unsalted butter, melted,
*   plus 2 tablespoons unsalted butter, cut into bits*

1½ cups lightly sweetened chunky applesauce,
*   preferably homemade from 3½ cups sliced*
*   peeled apples*

3 to 4 (1¼ pounds) cooking apples, peeled,
*   cored, and thinly sliced*

2½ to 3 tablespoons sugar

½ cup pale richly flavored jelly, such as apple,
*   quince, or yellow plum, melted*

Sprigs of unsprayed fruit, nut,
*   or rose leaves (not edible)*

Line an 11½-inch tart mold with the pastry dough, rolling over the edges to make a simple finish.

Slice the citrus fruits crosswise, peel included, ¼ inch thick; slice the end pieces into ¼-inch-wide strips. Discard the seeds. Place the slices in a small heavy-bottomed saucepan with the honey and liqueur. Bring to a boil, then reduce the heat, cover with the lid askew, and simmer until the fruits test thoroughly tender with a thin skewer, 20 to 30 minutes. Stir frequently. Remove from the heat and spread on a large plate to cool.

Heat the oven to 400°F. Brush the tart shell with the melted butter.

Divide the apples into 3 equal portions. Set 2 portions together in a single pile and 1 portion in another pile. Using the bottom of a tablespoon, smooth the applesauce over the bottom of the shell, then arrange the tangerine and lemon pieces with any syrup evenly over the applesauce. Top with the apple slices, overlapping them so they completely cover the citrus: Use the 2-portion pile in a circle around the outside edge, and then use the remaining pile to arrange an inner circle in the opposite direction. In the center, fit a few slices in a simple fan shape. Press the slices down into the fillings. Sprinkle the top with the sugar and then dot with the bits of butter.

Set the tart on a pizza pan or baking sheet and bake until the apple slices are thoroughly tender and almost translucent, 1¼ hours. Remove to a rack. Evenly spoon over the jelly glaze. Allow to cool to room temperature unmolding, sliding

onto a platter, and serving with a decorative flourish of leaves around the platter.

MAKE-AHEAD NOTE: See make-ahead notes for pastries on page 19. Serve the day you make it, although, truth to tell, it's still delicious the next day.

Viking Apple Tart

Thinly slice beautiful cooking apples and toss with a handful each of brown sugar and flour. Arrange in a partially baked Crisp Sweet Pastry shell (page 24), overlapping the slices. Bake about 15 minutes, then pour heavy cream evenly over the top. Continue to bake until tender. Sprinkle with nutmeg and serve warm on a platter rimmed with clusters of small red candles set alight.

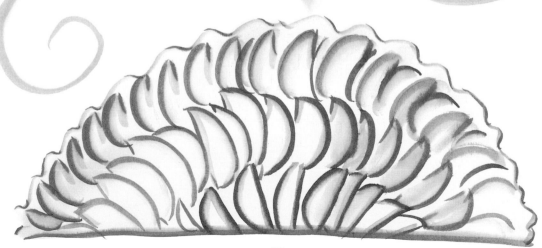

Tartlets of Brandied Gingery Mince

For Twelfth Night

These tartlets are rich and heavenly when made with prime ingredients. Don't use the candied peel at the supermarket. It's why people hate candied peel. Instead, go to a candy store and buy freshly candied peel that comes in strips. It'll make all the difference. If they're out of orange and have grapefruit peel, use it—it adds a perfumed flavor. If you can't buy either, use the same amount of finely shredded fresh orange zest, simmered first in sugar syrup (page 9) until tender. These are perfect for a holiday party as small servings among an assortment of desserts. You can make the tartlets any size you like from one-bite on up. Brandied gingery mincemeat is rich! Snifters of brandy make a splendid finish.

MAKES AT LEAST TWENTY 2½-INCH TARTLETS

1 cup (about 4½ ounces) walnut pieces, toasted

¼ cup (2 ounces) candied ginger, rinsed free of sugar and patted dry, plus 5 or more unrinsed large pieces for garnish

¼ cup (1½ ounces) candied orange peel

2⅔ cups (27 ounces) prepared mincemeat

2 tablespoons good brandy, or to taste

20 or more fully baked Crisp Sweet Pastry tartlet shells (page 24)

Unsprayed seasonal green sprigs (not edible)

Two weeks before serving, hand-chop the walnuts and rinsed pieces of ginger medium-fine and finely chop the candied peel. Place in a bowl with the mincemeat, mix well, then add the brandy. Blend thoroughly, then pack into a glass or ceramic vessel, cover tightly with plastic wrap, and let ripen in a cool place—not the refrigerator. Stir occasionally.

To serve, fill the tartlet shells and place on a platter. Cut slices of sugared candied ginger into quarters and set a piece on top of each tartlet. Decorate the platter with sprigs of the season. Don't use mistletoe, though, as it's poisonous.

MAKE-AHEAD NOTE: See make-ahead notes for pastries on page 19. The mincemeat must be prepared well in advance, and the filled tartlets hold up beautifully for a couple of days if kept in a cool place.

Scandinavian Napoleon Tartlets

Moistureproof the bottom of fully baked small Flaky Pastry tartlet shells (page 23) with melted red currant jelly. Fill half-full with chunky homemade applesauce flavored with vanilla. Cover and mound up with lightly sweetened whipped cream, then decorate with matchsticks of freshly candied orange peel and finely chopped toasted pistachios.

Fresh Sour Cherry Tart with Chocolate Crumbles

In Commemoration of George Washington's Truthfulness

One of my favorite combinations of flavors is cherries and chocolate. I'm also crazy about crumbles. Being a baker is rewarding. If you have a jar of vanilla sugar, omit the vanilla extract and use your vanilla sugar with the cherries. A little cherry heering to finish?

MAKES 8 SERVINGS

Crisp Sweet Pastry dough (page 24)

THE CHERRIES
5½ cups (scant 2½ pounds unpitted) pitted,
    stemmed, ripe red cherries
1⅓ cups granulated sugar
¼ teaspoon pure vanilla extract
2¾ tablespoons quick-cooking tapioca
Pinch of salt

THE CRUMBLES
Rounded ½ cup all-purpose flour
Rounded ½ cup turbinado or light brown sugar
Rounded ¼ cup unsweetened cocoa
Rounded ¼ cup (1½ ounces) ground almonds
¼ teaspoon cinnamon
6 tablespoons cold unsalted butter

½ cup tart cherry preserves or ½ cup sweet
    cherry preserves flavored with 1 teaspoon
    fresh orange juice
Sifted confectioners' sugar
8 small bunches tart cherries (with leaves,
    if possible)

Roll out the dough and line your tart mold.

To prepare the cherries, in a bowl, combine all the ingredients and toss them gently with a fork.

To prepare the crumbles, in a bowl, stir together the flour, sugar, cocoa, almonds, and cinnamon. Cut in the butter in small chips, then toss with your fingers until all is blended.

To bake, heat the oven to 425°F. Spread the preserves over the bottom of the tart shell to moistureproof it, and set it on a pizza pan or baking sheet. Arrange the cherry mixture in the shell, then strew the crumbles over the cherries with a light hand.

Bake until bubbly, 30 to 35 minutes. Remove from the pan and let cool on a rack. Unmold the tart and set on a doilied platter. Serve within a couple of hours. To serve, dust with sifted confectioners' sugar and heap the cherry bunches in the center. Use a bunch to decorate each slice.

MAKE-AHEAD NOTE: See make-ahead notes for pastries on page 19. The cherries and the crumbles can be prepared a couple of hours before composing the tart. Keep them in a cool place.

Tartlets of Glacé Clementines with White Chocolate

Clementines are mandarin oranges from North Africa, small and sweet, with few seeds. Of course, you can use any fine mandarin oranges. Within a few hours of serving, peel the clementines, remove as much white pith as possible, pull segments apart, and briefly dry them in a low oven. Boil a heavy sugar syrup (page 9, using double the amount of sugar) until a little dropped in cold water cracks. One by one, spear a segment of clementine with a toothpick and dip it into the syrup to coat with a thin shell. Set on an oiled tray, toothpick in place, until cool and dry. Remove the toothpicks with the help of a fork. To serve, make a bed of coarsely grated white chocolate on the bottom of small fully baked Crisp Sweet Pastry tartlet shells (page 24). Heap with the candied segments, border with grated white chocolate, and strew with candied violets.

Praline Mousse Tart with Raspberries and Dark Chocolate Lattice on a Toffee Crust

In Commemoration of Mary, Queen of Scots's Invention of Hopscotch

This tart is at once gay and regal—like my ancestor. After enjoying
it, knock back a little Drambuie in her honor.

MAKES 10 SERVINGS

THE PRALINE
A little unsalted butter
1 cup sugar
1 cup (3 ounces) sliced almonds

THE CUSTARD
2 packages (1 tablespoon plus about 1¼ teaspoons)
*   unflavored gelatin*
¼ cup cold brewed coffee
6 large egg yolks
1½ cups half-and-half
¼ cup sugar
1 teaspoon pure vanilla extract

Fully baked Toffee Crust (page 26)
1½ cups cold heavy cream
2 ounces bittersweet chocolate (page 9), chopped
*   into 1-inch pieces*
About 12 ounces fresh raspberries

To make the praline, butter a large, flat heatproof surface such as a baking sheet. In a large, heavy nonstick skillet, cook the sugar over medium heat until melted, stirring toward the end to prevent scorching and to break up lumps. It will be amber. (When you work with boiling sugar, be careful not to let any spatter onto your skin. Caramel is ferociously hot and will stick and burn painfully.) Add the almonds and stir over medium-low heat until the mixture is well blended and a rich amber. Immediately pour it onto the buttered surface, spreading it thinly with a wooden spoon. Let cool.

Break the cold praline into smallish pieces. Place 1 cup in a food processor or blender and grind to a powder. Grind the rest into crunchy bits small enough not to break a tooth. Combine the batches and set aside. You should have about 2 cups.

To make the custard, mix the gelatin and coffee in a small bowl and set aside to soften the gelatin. Turn the egg yolks into a small mixing bowl and whisk until blended. In a heavy-bottomed saucepan over medium heat, heat the half-and-half until a skin forms. Discard the skin. Slowly pour the half-and-half into the egg yolks, whisking vigorously. Whisk in the sugar and then the gelatin mixture, ignoring any lumps.

Pour this mixture back into the saucepan and set over low heat. Stir constantly and all across the bottom with a wooden spatula or spoon: Look at the back of the spoon now—the mixture is a thin *veil* across it. When the custard makes an opaque *coating* on the back of the spoon—run your finger through it and the track stays—it's cooked, 5 to 7 minutes. It won't be thick and custardy, as you might imagine, so don't overcook or it will curdle. Should you suddenly see specks of white in the custard, you've overcooked it: Pour it at once into a blender and whirl it until smooth. Remove the custard from the heat immediately and pour it through a fine-mesh sieve into a broad metal bowl or pot. Stir in the vanilla. Lay plastic wrap directly on the surface and refrigerate.

To compose the tart, set the tart shell on its base on a serving platter. In a large mixing bowl, whip the cream until very stiff. Melt the chocolate at half-power in the microwave, or in an uncovered heatproof bowl over barely simmering water. Stir until blended, then keep warm and soft.

Now you want to soften the gelled mixture. Holding the metal bowl over a very low burner, very briefly beat with a portable mixer or whisk until the custard softens to the consistency of unbeaten egg white—gloppy thick but pourable and velvety smooth. Remove from the heat. If it melted too much and is runny, chill it a few minutes until it reaches the consistency just described. Sprinkle the praline over the custard and fold it in thoroughly with a large rubber spatula. Add the whipped cream and fold in thoroughly.

Heap this mousse onto the crust, then quickly smooth the top and sides with a spatula to give it the shape of a cake. It can firm up in minutes. Use a small spoon to drizzle the chocolate in a hopscotchlike grid on top (or simply make squares). Let the chocolate lines be wonderfully crude. Set a raspberry in the center of each square, then strew the rest of the berries around the platter. Keep cool until serving, then cut into wedges.

MAKE-AHEAD NOTE: See make-ahead notes for pastries on page 19. You can put the elements of this tart together over a couple of days. Praline keeps for months wrapped airtight in the refrigerator or freezer. The custard mixture can be prepared a day in advance. The heavy cream can be whipped a couple of hours before being folded into the custard. Whisk it lightly until fluffy just before using. The mousse (combined custard mixture and whipped cream) must be smoothed into place immediately, as it can set in 10 minutes. Kept in a cold place (preferably not the refrigerator), the finished tart can wait up to 2 hours without harm.

Pineapple Honeyed Toffee Tart

This is lovely for Passover (grind the nuts without flour). Just before serving, cover a baked Toffee Crust (page 26) with mounds of freshly made pineapple ice (just freeze lightly sweetened pineapple purée in a flat pan, stirring occasionally, and serve when a tinkly crush). Strew the ice with toasted sliced almonds, grated bittersweet chocolate, a little chopped candied ginger, and drizzle with warmed honey. Crown with the trimmed top of the pineapple.

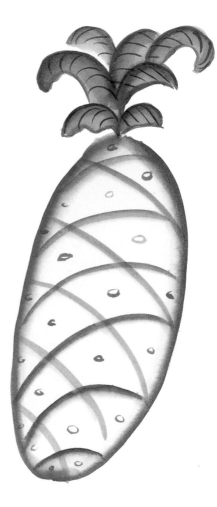

French Marbled Cheese Tart with Pomegranate Sauce

Although a cousin of New York cheesecake, this tart is distinctly European: The shell isn't crumbs but a crisp pastry, and the filling isn't light and creamy but rich and dense. You'll find it irresistible. The sauce is a brilliant touch of autumn. When pomegranates aren't in season, you can purée and strain frozen raspberries for a scarlet sauce. The marbling beneath the scarlet is beautiful and pomegranate's tang is marvelous with chocolate. So is crème de cacao—sip some after coffee. If you can, buy whole-milk ricotta from an Italian delicatessen. If you can't and the cheese from the supermarket is drippy, turn it into a sieve and drain off the excess moisture (allow 6 to 8 hours). At the very least, blot the cheese dry with a towel. A little settling and cracking is unavoidable in cheesecake, and not a concern. But here's a secret to cheesecake success: Don't whisk or beat the batter. Instead stir it gently with a large rubber spatula (the larger the surface of the tool, the more batter is blended in one stroke). Air beaten into the batter makes it rise in the oven, which, because cheesecake hasn't the wherewithal to stay up, dooms it to falling, cracking, and being dry when cooled. Have all ingredients at 70°F. Although directions are detailed, this is a simple tart to make.

MAKES 8 SERVINGS

Fully baked Crisp Sweet Pastry shell (page 24)

THE VANILLA BATTER

2 pounds premium-quality ricotta cheese,
*   drained if necessary*

½ cup sugar

1 tablespoon pure vanilla extract

5 large eggs

½ cup heavy cream

THE CHOCOLATE BATTER

5 tablespoons unsweetened cocoa (not Dutch
*   process), sifted if lumpy*

2 tablespoons sugar

1 tablespoon heavy cream

1 teaspoon pure vanilla extract

1 tablespoon all-purpose flour

THE POMEGRANATE SAUCE

4 large (about 3 pounds) pomegranates

2 tablespoons strained fresh orange juice

¼ cup sugar

Pinch of salt

2 tablespoons cornstarch

4 tablespoons cold water

1 tablespoon (from 2 packages) unflavored gelatin

Heat the oven to 350°F. Set the shell in its mold on a pizza pan or baking pan.

To make the vanilla batter, in a large bowl, use a large rubber spatula to blend the ricotta, sugar, and vanilla. Add the eggs two at a time and then the one, stirring until blended after each addition. Blend in the cream.

In another bowl, combine 2 cups of the vanilla batter with all the ingredients for the chocolate batter. Stir until smooth. Slowly sprinkle the flour over the top of the remaining vanilla batter, stirring it in after each sprinkling.

Smooth half of the chocolate batter over the bottom of the shell. Drop half of the vanilla batter in spoonfuls here and there onto the chocolate. Then, using the back of a spoon, smooth it over in a layer. Repeat with the rest of the chocolate batter and then the rest of the vanilla batter. For the marbling, at one side of the tart, drop the tip of a table knife down through the batter *not quite all the way to the bottom,* then pull the knife through the batter straight to the other side. Or you can pull it in a zigzag or any pattern you like. Do this only 3 or 4 times through the batter. Marble it too much and the pattern will be muddy.

Bake until you can smell the chocolate and a knife thrust just this side of the center comes out clean, 40 to 45 minutes. Don't overbake. Slide onto a rack and let cool as usual.

Meanwhile, make the pomegranate sauce. While you can ream it like an orange, the way to get the sweetest juice from a pomegranate is to work in a big bowl, removing all the white membrane and turning the seeds into a blender. Whirl them on "grind," then strain through a fine-mesh sieve, pressing out every drop of juice. You should have 2 cups juice.

In a saucepan, combine the pomegranate and orange juices with the sugar and salt. Bring to a simmer over medium heat. Meanwhile, blend the cornstarch with 2 tablespoons of the water in one dish, and soften the gelatin in the remaining 2 tablespoons water in another.

Whisk the cornstarch into the simmering juice, turn the heat to low, and simmer, stirring, for 2 minutes. Remove from the heat and blend in the gelatin mixture. Pass the sauce through a fine-mesh sieve, lay plastic wrap directly on top so a skin won't form, and let cool. You should have about 2 cups.

Remove the tart ring but leave the base. Set the tart on its platter. Just before serving, smooth ½ cup of the pomegranate sauce over the cheese, filling any cracks. Pour the remaining sauce into a bowl. To serve, spoon 3 tablespoons sauce around each slice.

MAKE-AHEAD NOTE: See make-ahead notes for pastries on page 19. Always best the day of baking, this tart is remarkably delicious the next day—just wait to glaze it as noted. You can prepare the sauce a day in advance.

Bourbon'd Bittersweet Chocolate Walnut Tart

For Derby Day

My grandmother was mad about bourbon, the horses, chocolate, and rich desserts, in that order. A crunchy inch of the densest, nuttiest dark chocolate you ever ate—with a hint of Kentucky's finest—this is for her. There are three ways to enjoy it. With a simple drift of confectioners' sugar over the top, you can savor this close-to-confection purely. With a plop or piping of unsweetened whipped cream, there's lightness to balance richness. A scoop of vanilla ice cream on top of each slice matches the creamy chocolate beneath. I vote for ice cream. Cups of continental-style coffee are boon companions. On the subject of turning the chocolate and walnuts into morsels: When walnut halves are broken by hand, there are no powdery nuts to cloud the custard. But a little ground chocolate in the custard flavors it, so you do want to chop the chocolate in a food processor or blender.

MAKES 10 SERVINGS

Unbaked Crisp Sweet Pastry shell (page 24)

8 tablespoons (4 ounces) unsalted butter, melted

1 cup firmly packed light brown sugar

Slightly rounded ¼ cup cornstarch

3 large eggs

¼ cup light corn syrup

7 tablespoons bourbon

1¾ cups (5¼ ounces) hand-broken walnut bits
(¼ to ½ inch), toasted

1¼ cups (7 ounces) machine-chopped bits
(¼ to ½ inch) bittersweet chocolate (page 9)

1 tablespoon unsweetened cocoa

SOME OPTIONAL FINISHES

A little sifted confectioners' sugar

1 cup cold heavy cream, beaten until stiff

1¼ quarts vanilla ice cream, in 10 scoops set
around the outside edge of the tart

Moistureproof the pastry shell by brushing it with about 1 tablespoon of the melted butter, then refrigerate until needed.

Position 1 rack on the lowest oven shelf and 1 rack in the middle of the oven and heat to 425°F. In a large bowl, use your hands to rub the brown sugar and cornstarch together until blended and there are no lumps. Add the eggs and stir with a wooden spoon until smooth. One by one, blend in the corn syrup, bourbon, and the remaining melted butter, stirring until smooth after each addition. Sprinkle the walnuts and chocolate evenly over the egg mixture, then stir until blended.

Set the tart on a pizza pan or baking sheet. Smooth the mixture into the shell, evenly distributing the nuts, chocolate, and custard. Turn the cocoa into a fine-mesh sieve, and shake it evenly over the top. Set the pan on the bottom rack and bake for 15 minutes. Move the pan to the middle rack, lower the heat to 350°F, and bake until a knife slipped into the custard a couple of inches from the center comes out clean, 15 to 20 minutes. Don't overbake—the custard keeps cooking out of the oven. Unmold and cool on a rack. Serve on a platter at room temperature with the desired finish.

MAKE-AHEAD NOTE: Although sensational the day of baking, it's possible this tart is even better the next day.

Mexican Chocolate Banana Whipped Cream Tart

Spread melted bittersweet chocolate on the bottom of a fully baked Crisp Sweet Pastry shell (page 24). Just before serving, cover with sliced bananas, drizzle with more melted chocolate, cover with whipped cream, strew with toasted sliced almonds and fine shreds of orange zest, and dust with cinnamon.

Table of Equivalents

The exact equivalents in the following tables have been rounded for convenience.

US/UK

oz = ounce
lb = pound
in = inch
ft = foot
fl oz = fluid ounce
qt = quart

METRIC

g = gram
kg = kilogram
mm = millimeter
cm = centimeter
ml = milliliter
l = liter

WEIGHTS

US/UK	metric
1 oz	30 g
2 oz	60 g
3 oz	90 g
4 oz (¼ lb)	125 g
5 oz (⅓ lb)	155 g
6 oz	185 g
7 oz	220 g
8 oz (½ lb)	250 g
10 oz	315 g
12 oz (¾ lb)	375 g
14 oz	440 g
16 oz (1 lb)	500 g
1½ lb	750 g
2 lb	1 kg
3 lb	1.5 kg

OVEN TEMPERATURES

Fahrenheit	Celsius	gas
250	120	½
275	140	1
300	150	2
325	160	3
350	180	4
375	190	5
400	200	6
425	220	7
450	320	8
475	240	9
500	260	10

LIQUIDS

US	metric	UK
2 tbl	30 ml	1 fl oz
¼ cup	60 ml	2 fl oz
⅓ cup	80 ml	3 fl oz
½ cup	125 ml	4 fl oz
⅔ cup	160 ml	5 fl oz
¾ cup	180 ml	6 fl oz
1 cup	250 ml	8 fl oz
1½ cups	375 ml	12 fl oz
2 cups	500 ml	16 fl oz
4 cups/1 qt	1 liter	32 fl oz

LENGTH MEASUREMENTS

⅛ in	3 mm
¼ in	6 mm
½ in	12 mm
1 in	2.5 cm
2 in	5 cm
3 in	7.5 cm
4 in	10 cm
5 in	13 cm
6 in	15 cm
7 in	18 cm
8 in	20 cm
9 in	23 cm
10 in	24 cm
11 in	28 cm
12 in/1 ft	30 cm

Equivalents for Commonly Used Ingredients

ALL-PURPOSE (PLAIN) PLOUR/DRIED BREAD CRUMBS/CHOPPED NUTS

¼ cup	1 oz	30 g
⅓ cup	1½ oz	45 g
½ cup	2 oz	60 g
¾ cup	3 oz	90 g
1 cup	4 oz	125 g
1½ cups	6 oz	185 g
2 cups	8 oz	250 g

WHOLE-WHEAT (WHOLEMEAL) FLOUR

3 tbl	1 oz	30 g
½ cup	2 oz	60 g
⅔ cup	3 oz	90 g
1 cup	4 oz	125 g
1¼ cups	5 oz	155 g
1⅔ cups	7 oz	210 g
1¾ cups	8 oz	250 g

BROWN SUGAR

¼ cup	1½ oz	45 g
½ cup	3 oz	90 g
¾ cup	4 oz	125 g
1 cup	5½ oz	170 g
1½ cups	8 oz	250 g
2 cups	10 oz	315 g

WHITE SUGAR

¼ cup	2 oz	60 g
⅓ cup	3 oz	90 g
½ cup	4 oz	125 g
¾ cup	6 oz	185 g
1 cup	8 oz	250 g
1½ cups	12 oz	375 g
2 cups	1 lb	500 g

RAISINS/CURRANTS/ SEMOLINA

¼ cup	1 oz	30 g
⅓ cup	2 oz	60 g
½ cup	3 oz	90 g
¾ cup	4 oz	125 g
1 cup	5 oz	155 g

LONG-GRAIN RICE/ CORNMEAL

⅓ cup	2 oz	60 g
½ cup	2½ oz	75 g
¾ cup	4 oz	125 g
1 cup	5 oz	155 g
1½ cups	8 oz	250 g

DRIED BEANS

¼ cup	1½ oz	45 g
⅓ cup	2 oz	60 g
½ cup	3 oz	90 g
¾ cup	5 oz	155 g
1 cup	6 oz	185 g
1¼ cups	8 oz	250 g
1½ cups	12 oz	375 g

ROLLED OATS

⅓ cup	1 oz	30 g
⅔ cup	2 oz	60 g
1 cup	3 oz	90 g
1½ cups	4 oz	125 g
2 cups	5 oz	155 g

JAM/HONEY

2 tbl	2 oz	60 g
¼ cup	3 oz	90 g
½ cup	5 oz	155 g
¾ cup	8 oz	250 g
1 cup	11 oz	345 g

GRATED PARMESAN/ ROMANO CHEESE

¼ cup	1 oz	30 g
½ cup	2 oz	60 g
¾ cup	3 oz	90 g
1 cup	4 oz	125 g
1⅓ cups	5 oz	155 g
2 cups	7 oz	220 g